Nuclear Family Values, Extended Family Lives: The Power of Race, Class, and Gender

Natalia Sarkisian and Naomi Gerstel

When discussing families, social commentators typically focus on mothers, fathers, and young children. This book shows how this emphasis on marriage and the nuclear family—with its exclusion of the extended family—is narrow and misses much of family life, especially the familial experiences of women, racial/ethnic minorities, and low wage workers and the poor for whom extended families are centrally important. While many argue that marriage is the foundation of the community, this book shows that marriage detracts from other social ties. Inattention to extended families reduces the power of social policy to improve the lives of Americans.

Natalia Sarkisian is Associate Professor of Sociology at Boston College. Her interests include family sociology, race, gender, and class, aging and the life course, and quantitative methods. Her research, published in *Social Forces*, *American Sociological Review*, the *Journal of Marriage and Family*, *Contexts*, and *Family Relations*, examines variation in kin and community ties by race/ethnicity, gender, age, and marital status, and explores the structural circumstances and cultural values that may account for this variation.

Naomi Gerstel is Distinguished University Professor in the Department of Sociology at the University of Massachusetts, Amherst. Her most recent articles have examined the ways class and gender shape work hours, effects of class, race, marriage, and women's employment on families and caregiving, labor union policies, and the Family and Medical Leave Act. Her co-authored and co-edited books include *Commuter Marriage*, *Families at Work*, *Families and Work*, and *Public Sociology*.

 THE SOCIAL ISSUES COLLECTION™

Framing 21st Century Social Issues

The goal of this new, unique Series is to offer readable, teachable "thinking frames" on today's social problems and social issues by leading scholars. These are available for view on http://routledge.customgateway.com/routledge-social-issues.html.

For instructors teaching a wide range of courses in the social sciences, the Routledge *Social Issues Collection* now offers the best of both worlds: originally written short texts that provide "overviews" to important social issues *as well as* teachable excerpts from larger works previously published by Routledge and other presses.

As an instructor, click to the website to view the library and decide how to build your custom anthology and which thinking frames to assign. Students can choose to receive the assigned materials in print and/or electronic formats at an affordable price.

Available

Body Problems
Running and Living Long in a Fast-Food Society
Ben Agger

Sex, Drugs, and Death
Addressing Youth Problems in American Society
Tammy Anderson

The Stupidity Epidemic
Worrying About Students, Schools, and America's Future
Joel Best

Empire Versus Democracy
The Triumph of Corporate and Military Power
Carl Boggs

Contentious Identities
Ethnic, Religious, and Nationalist Conflicts in Today's World
Daniel Chirot

The Future of Higher Education
Dan Clawson and Max Page

Waste and Consumption
Capitalism, the Environment, and the Life of Things
Simonetta Falasca-Zamponi

Rapid Climate Change
Causes, Consequences, and Solutions
Scott G. McNall

The Problem of Emotions in Societies
Jonathan H. Turner

Outsourcing the Womb
Race, Class, and Gestational Surrogacy in a Global Market
France Winddance Twine

Changing Times for Black Professionals
Adia Harvey Wingfield

Nuclear Family Values, Extended Family Lives
The Power of Race, Class, and Gender

Natalia Sarkisian

Boston College

Noami Gerstel

University of Massachusetts, Amherst

Routledge
Taylor & Francis Group

NEW YORK AND LONDON

First published 2012
by Routledge
711 Third Avenue, New York, NY 10017

Simultaneously published in the UK
by Routledge
2 Park Square, Milton Park, Abingdon, Oxon OX14 4RN

Routledge is an imprint of the Taylor & Francis Group, an informa business

Library of Congress Cataloging in Publication Data
Sarkisian, Natalia.
Nuclear family values, extended family lives : the power of race, class, and gender /
Natalia Sarkisian, Naomi Gerstel.
p. cm. —(Framing 21st century social issues)
1. Nuclear families—United States. 2. Families—United States. I. Gerstel, Naomi.
II. Title.
HQ536.S3336 2011
306.85'50973—dc23
2011039697

ISBN: 978-0-415-80841-5 (pbk)
ISBN: 978-0-203-14197-7 (ebk)

Typeset in Garamond and Gill Sans
by EvS Communication Networx, Inc.

Printed and bound in the United States of America on acid-free paper.

Contents

Series Foreword

The world in the early 21st century is beset with problems—a troubled economy, global warming, oil spills, religious and national conflict, poverty, HIV, health problems associated with sedentary lifestyles. Virtually no nation is exempt, and everyone, even in affluent countries, feels the impact of these global issues.

Since its inception in the 19th century, sociology has been the academic discipline dedicated to analyzing social problems. It is still so today. Sociologists offer not only diagnoses; they glimpse solutions, which they then offer to policy makers and citizens who work for a better world. Sociology played a major role in the civil rights movement during the 1960s in helping us to understand racial inequalities and prejudice, and it can play a major role today as we grapple with old and new issues.

This series builds on the giants of sociology, such as Weber, Durkheim, Marx, Parsons, and Mills. It uses their frames, and newer ones, to focus on particular issues of contemporary concern. These books are about the nuts and bolts of social problems, but they are equally about the frames through which we analyze these problems. It is clear by now that there is no single correct way to view the world, but only paradigms, models, which function as lenses through which we peer. For example, in analyzing oil spills and environmental pollution, we can use a frame that views such outcomes as unfortunate results of a reasonable effort to harvest fossil fuels. "Drill, baby, drill" sometimes involves certain costs as pipelines rupture and oil spews forth. Or we could analyze these environmental crises as inevitable outcomes of our effort to dominate nature in the interest of profit. The first frame would solve oil spills with better environmental protection measures and clean-ups, while the second frame would attempt to prevent them altogether, perhaps shifting away from the use of petroleum and natural gas and toward alternative energies that are "green."

These books introduce various frames such as these for viewing social problems. They also highlight debates between social scientists who frame problems differently. The books suggest solutions, both on the macro and micro levels. That is, they suggest what new policies might entail, and they also identify ways in which people, from the ground level, can work toward a better world, changing themselves and their lives and families and providing models of change for others.

Readers do not need an extensive background in academic sociology to benefit from these books. Each book is student-friendly in that we provide glossaries of terms for the uninitiated that are keyed to bolded terms in the text. Each chapter ends with questions for further thought and discussion. The level of each book is accessible to undergraduate students, even as these books offer sophisticated and innovative analyses.

When discussing families, social commentators typically focus on mothers, fathers, and young children. Naomi Gerstel and Natalia Sarkisian show how this emphasis on marriage and the nuclear family—with its exclusion of the extended family—is narrow and misses much of family life, especially the familial experiences of women, racial/ethnic minorities, and low-wage workers and the poor for whom extended families are centrally important. While many argue that marriage is the foundation of American communities, this book demonstrates that a narrow concept of marriage detracts from other social ties. In this important book, the authors broaden the concept of "family," both reflecting the diversity of American families and suggesting policy implications that would protect and nurture these diverse family forms.

Preface

When discussing families, politicians and sociologists alike typically focus on parents and their young children. They are especially likely to emphasize issues related to marriage, highlight the role of fathers, and promote the importance of a two-parent nuclear family. This book argues that such rhetoric is a poor reflection of the everyday lives of many Americans for whom family includes aging parents, grown up children, adult siblings, aunts, uncles, cousins, grandparents, and grandchildren. We question the focus on nuclear family by highlighting the roles that these extended family members play in the lives of Americans. We demonstrate that many Americans spend substantial amounts of time with their relatives, frequently rely on extended family members for help, and provide assistance in return.

The book argues that this narrow emphasis on marriage and the nuclear family, with its exclusion of the extended family, is particularly likely to overlook family experiences of some groups of Americans—those that are already disadvantaged by racial/ethnic, gender, and economic inequalities. It overlooks women's experiences as they are more likely than men to do the work of maintaining ties to relatives and serve as the glue for extended family and community ties. It ignores the familial experiences of many racial/ethnic minorities for whom extended families are centrally important. And it advances a vision of families that dismisses the social resources especially critical to the survival strategies of those in need—low-wage workers and the poor.

This book also addresses another facet of the popular rhetoric on families—that emphasizing the role of marriage as social glue. For many social critics and observers, not only is the nuclear family the basic unit of society, but marriage is the foundation of the community. Marriage, to them, is the endangered basis of a healthy society, whose fragility threatens children and adults as well as the broader community. In contrast, we demonstrate that in many ways, marriage actually separates men and women from other social connections and therefore detracts from ties to extended families and broader communities. These isolating effects of marriage are felt across race and class, but because those with fewer economic resources are more likely to rely on extended family, these effects of marriage are particularly costly to them.

The book concludes with an examination of the impact of nuclear family rhetoric on social policy. In line with this rhetoric, many social policies, including family and medical leave policies, Medicaid, gay and lesbian marriage, welfare reform, and policies on grandparents, are geared towards the nuclear family. We argue that this inattention to the extended family reduces the effectiveness, reach, and potential power of family policy. We conclude that not only does a focus on marriage and the nuclear family miss a great deal of family life and denigrate poor and minority families, but it also facilitates social policies that discriminate against women, people of color, and the poor and thereby reduces the power of social policy to improve lives of Americans.

1: The Widespread Focus on Nuclear Families

❦

The family is the basic unit of American society. Family values are at the core of American culture. Or so many social commentators have said for at least a century. However, the family that they argue is the basic unit of American society is not just any family. It is the **nuclear family**, consisting of a mother, a father, and their young children still living at home. Take no less a figure than Barack Obama. When he talks about the value of families (which he does fairly often), he—like most other politicians—tends to focus on the nuclear family. Recently he said: "Of all the rocks upon which we build our lives, we are reminded today that family is the most important" (Obama 2008). Obama elaborated by saying: "too many fathers are missing" and pointed out that half of all Black children live in single parent households. He concluded by saying: "the foundations of our community are weaker because of it."

The irony of Obama's emphasis on the intact nuclear family is that it flies in the face of his own much celebrated experience as a man who attended an Ivy League college and a prestigious law school before becoming senator and president but nonetheless was raised by a single mother and grandparents, with a famously absent father.

Obama's much cited defense of the nuclear family but his rare mention of the **extended family** contradicts his current experience as well. Little has been made of the fact that he now lives with his mother-in-law, so the White House contains an extended family. Several months after Obama made these remarks about the nuclear family, he discussed families at the 2010 Whitehouse Forum on Workplace Flexibility, emphasizing not only taking care of children but also the importance of elderly parents giving and getting care. He even mentioned, with a smile, the importance of having Michelle's mother living in the White House. But this was unusual; his major focus is on the nuclear family, especially fatherhood, as evidenced by his recent National Fatherhood Initiative and the National Responsible Fatherhood Clearinghouse (NRFC).

Just like Obama, when talking about family obligations and solidarities, politicians on both the left and the right typically focus on the ties between spouses and between parents and their children, especially when those children are young. Indeed, Wikipedia (the most popular online encyclopedia) provides the following definition in the article on family values: "Family values are political and social beliefs that hold the nuclear family to be the essential ethical and moral unit of society" (Wikipedia 2011).

Conservative politicians are the ones who use references to family values most often. Take, for example, Focus on the Family, the group founded by evangelical James Dobson. This group emphasizes that we need to return to what Dobson calls the "traditional family." What is that family? Husband and wife, parents and young children. It is not just that Dobson leaves out single parents and gay parents; he also leaves out adult children, siblings, aunts, uncles, cousins, and grandparents.

Although "family values" remain central in conservative rhetoric, this term is increasingly popular among liberals as well. When discussing family values, Democrats often emphasize the acceptance of single-parent families and same-sex marriages, the needs of "working families" for minimum wage increases and the maintenance of Medicare, childcare and parent-friendly employment laws such as job leaves for medical emergencies involving children, as well as sex education and access to contraception and abortion. Although such liberal definitions of family values differ from those used by conservatives, they are still limited in important ways. Ties between adult children and aging parents, grandparents and grandchildren, adult siblings, uncles and aunts, nieces and nephews are still missing from this rhetoric of family values.

Indeed, extended families rarely appear in the widespread discussions of family values on either the conservative or the liberal side. Even though the U.S. census defines a family as those individuals related by blood, marriage or adoption who reside together—imposing a co-residence requirement but not excluding extended kin entirely, a recent press release from the U.S. Census Bureau (2010) addresses the recession's effects on families even more narrowly, focusing solely on husbands, wives, and their young children. There were no parents of adult children, no sisters or brothers, no aunts, no uncles, no grandparents (although, as this book will show, these are the very people on whom those who lose their jobs often rely).

In contrast to the rhetoric of politicians and the assumptions of governmental agencies, few Americans define family values in terms of the traditional nuclear family. In one poll, only 2 percent of women and 1 percent of men defined family values that way. In contrast, 52 percent of women and 42 percent of men thought family values meant "loving, taking care of, and supporting each other" (Galinsky et al. 1995).

This notion of family values reflects Americans' evolving ideas of what constitutes a family. These ideas are rapidly moving away from simply endorsing the nuclear family; instead, they are becoming more inclusive—referring not only to the relations of husbands and wives or parents and their young children but also to the attachment and caregiving among a wide range of extended family members and **fictive kin**.

Indeed, recent surveys show that Americans' definitions of family are becoming more expansive over time (Powell et al. 2010). According to Powell and his colleagues, these changes can be seen most clearly in the shifting views concerning same sex families: The majority of Americans now say that gays and lesbians, especially those who share a home and have young children, count as family. Ironically, this reevaluation coincides with another trend—gays and lesbians increasingly emphasize that they too can and should partake of the marital/nuclear family template by legalizing their marriages and having children. This has all but replaced the emphasis of earlier cohorts of gays and lesbians on "families we choose" (Weston 1991)—a view that entails much broader understandings of families and kinship.

For about the last half century, family definitions have been a target of debates in the social sciences as well. Some scholars have adopted a structural definition—they emphasized family composition, arguing that a family consists of a man, a woman, and their biological children sharing a residence. Others prefer functional definitions, focusing on tasks such as reproduction, socialization of children, or economic support and then defining the family as the unit that not only does, but has to perform these functions (Parsons and Bales 1955; Popenoe 1993). Yet others assume a postmodern, constructionist approach, arguing that a monolithic notion of the family does not exist; for them, family encompasses a diversity of structures, functions, and processes and its meaning is socially constructed and depends on the context (Stacey 1997; 2011; Gubrium and Holstein 1990). Indeed, as we saw in the example of Obama, the same person can define family differently depending on the situation.

Nevertheless, like most political pundits, most social scientists focus on marriage and the nuclear family. Most articles in academic journals that look at families look only at marriage (or its absence as in cohabitation or divorce) and parents with young children at home. The top journal in sociology (the *American Sociological Review*) and the most cited journal in family studies (the *Journal of Marriage and Family*) both contain articles looking at couples—cohabiting, communicating, cleaning, having sex or not, quarreling and breaking up—and both have even more articles on parents and their children—sometimes very young and sometimes adolescent, sometimes living in two parent families, sometimes in single parent families. But neither journal has many articles looking at extended families. For instance, over the last half decade, only 12 percent of articles in the *Journal of Marriage and Family* focused on relationships with relatives, whether elderly parents, adult children, siblings, grandparents, grandchildren, aunts and uncles, or cousins.

This book shows how the emphasis on nuclear family—with its exclusion of the extended family—is narrow, even deleterious, and misses much of family life. It misses numerous **kinkeeping** activities that many Americans undertake to maintain connections with their relatives: Phone calls, emails, visits, holiday cards and gifts, organization of family gatherings, mediation of family conflicts. It also misses all the **carework** that takes place in extended families—that is, all the help that Americans give to and get from their relatives. People often rely on extended families in times of crisis—when they experience major illness or disability, live through a divorce or widowhood, have financial problems or legal problems, face unemployment or spousal abuse, or lose their homes. Upon their arrival in this country, many immigrants rely on relatives for housing, employment, financial help, and social networks—in fact, many initially settle near their relatives, creating a phenomenon known as chain migration. Americans also turn to relatives when they want to celebrate—extended families help organize and finance weddings, birthdays, quinceañeras, bar and bat mitzvahs. And relatives help each other on a day-to-day basis—watching each other's children, helping with shopping or tasks around the house, giving a ride, offering advice and emotional support. This book argues that if we focus solely on marriage and nuclear family, we miss these family experiences.

First, in Chapters II and III, we will show that the focus on marriage and the nuclear family is a narrow view that ignores the familial practices and experiences of many Americans, particularly those of women and racial/ethnic minorities for whom extended families are centrally important. Second, in Chapter IV, we will show that an emphasis on the nuclear family may actually promulgate a vision of family life that dismisses the very social resources and community ties that are especially critical to the survival strategies of those in need. Third, in Chapter V, in contrast to those who have argued that marriage is the foundation of the community, we suggest that marriage actually detracts from social integration and ties to broader communities. Finally, turning to social policy in Chapter VI, we suggest that the focus on marriage and the nuclear family and the inattention to the extended family reduces the power and reach of social policy.

DISCUSSION QUESTIONS

1. How do you define family? What is your "ideal" family? Does your family meet the criteria of your "ideal" family? Where do you think your notions of "ideal" family come from?
2. How do notions of family values used by conservative and liberal politicians differ? What do they share?
3. How do the ideas about family values used in political rhetoric differ from those that regular Americans hold?

II: The Realities of Family Life

Extended Families and Gender

Newspapers and TV routinely present images of people balancing family and work, but these are almost always images of paid work and nuclear families. Mothers with young children appear quite frequently in such media stories. One such story that appeared recently in the *New York Times Magazine* generated heated debates. In this story, titled "The Opt-Out Revolution," *New York Times* correspondent Lisa Belkin (2003) argued that upper-class mothers with good careers increasingly choose to forego these careers to "go back home." Many saw this story as misleading, suggesting that statistical analyses do not support Belkin's assertion that highly educated mothers are abandoning high-powered jobs (Boushey 2005). Sociologist Pamela Stone probed this phenomenon in more depth in her book *Opting Out: Why Women Really Quit Careers and Head Home* (2007) and concluded that high-achieving mothers quit work only as a last resort. They "choose" to leave because their employers do not allow the flexibility they need, and because their partners are unwilling or unable to be flexible in their careers. Some of these women, according to Stone, also "found themselves marginalized and stigmatized, negatively reinforced for trying to hold onto their careers after becoming mothers" (Stone 2007: 19).

While mothers have been the primary target of work/family discussions in the media, fathers also increasingly appear. Another *New York Times* article titled "Now, Dad Feels as Stressed as Mom" argues that "fathers are now struggling just as much—and sometimes even more—than mothers in trying to fulfill their responsibilities at home and in the office" (Parker-Pope 2010).

While fathers are increasingly appearing in the work-life discussions, extended family members are notoriously absent from media stories about families and paid work. Grandmothers and grandfathers, uncles and aunts, adult brothers and sisters making the work/family balance possible are almost never featured in the media—we rarely find out about either the burdens they generate or the help they provide.

Much of the discussion of families and work, while sensitive to gender inequalities in nuclear families and jobs, ignores the work necessary to maintain extended family ties—both the care received from and the care provided to extended family members. The omission of such care and kinkeeping labor from discussions of family/work balance introduces crucial gender biases as it overlooks much of the unpaid work that women do.

To be sure, men also do such work. Nevertheless, there is much evidence that women are—compared to men—keepers of the extended family.

Gender Differences in Kinkeeping and Extended Family Carework

In the contemporary United States, women are more involved with relatives than men. Women keep in touch with relatives far more often than do men. Women usually organize family celebrations, invite family members to visit, and cook holiday dinners. Women also spend significantly more time giving hands-on help to relatives and friends than do men. To put it quite starkly, such caregiving adds *more than an extra week's work to women's monthly load*. This labor is a "third shift" (Gerstel 2000) because so many women do it in addition to the "first shift" of jobs and what Arlie Hochschild (1997) calls the "second shift" of housework and childcare. What constitutes this third shift?

One large component is assistance to elderly parents. Although a substantial portion of both women and men spend 30 or more hours per month providing care to parents and parents-in-law, women are twice as likely as men to do so (Heymann 2000). Studies show that women are more likely than men to assist their own parents and, when married, more likely than their husbands to assist their spouses' parents (Walker 2001). Gender differences are also substantial in the help parents give to their adult children. Such help can be offered on a daily basis, in times of crisis or in connection with celebrations. Gender differences are particularly pronounced with regard to grandchildren: Grandmothers are much more likely than grandfathers to help out. Women also see and help their siblings more than men (Campbell, Connidis, and Davies 1999). Having at least one sister in the family means siblings will interact more with one another (White and Riedmann 1992).

Studies find that women do a large share of what is conventionally thought of as "men's" work, but men do little of "women's" work. Stated bluntly, these findings suggest there is very little *division* of labor as far as caregiving is concerned: Overall, women give far more care to close and distant relatives than do men.

Yet, the work done for extended kin and for others outside of one's own household is often invisible or sentimentalized. That is, it is often not perceived as work and is ignored in discussions of paid and unpaid labor. Frequently, the emotional component of this type of work is the reason why people do not perceive this as work—people see caregiving as something women do "out of love" for their relatives and worry that to call it work is to demean it. Similar bias exists with regard to women's care for nuclear families, yet this bias has been challenged much more extensively. Thus, the omission of kin work from family studies and from public discussions devalues women's work: It conceals the hard labor that goes into maintaining families.

Why Do Women and Men Differ?

Biology

Many people see any and all differences between women and men as rooted in biology. Men and women do have different reproductive functions, so it is easy to believe that this is what causes them to differ in a lot of other ways. It is especially easy to believe that differences between women and men are biological when it comes to family matters—after all, family is where reproduction typically takes place. This focus on biology when explaining differences between women and men is called **essentialism** because this theory attributes gender differences to the essential gender dichotomy rooted in *biology* (for a review, see Epstein 1988).

Essentialist theories say that gender differences in caregiving are bound up with the biological make-up of women and men. Essentialists view these differences as deep and tenacious, prevalent in all societies across all time. Essentialist theories used to be very popular in social science in the mid-twentieth century but they have been challenged and criticized ever since, although recent interest in genetics and biology has revived gender essentialism to a certain extent.

Psychology

Another common theory of gender differences attributes them to *psychological differences* created by early childhood experiences. One classic explanation, developed by Nancy Chodorow (1978), uses psychoanalytic theory to explain why women are predisposed to nurturing labor. Both boys and girls develop strong connection to and identification with their mothers. Whereas girls are never forced to sever that connection, boys have to renounce their identification with the mother in order to develop a masculine identity. In that painful process, boys' relational capacity is greatly reduced, and they learn to devalue and reject everything associated with femininity. As a result, adult men unconsciously avoid nurturing labor, whereas adult women seek it.

Like essentialist arguments, however, this psychoanalytic explanation mostly emphasizes uniformity among women and among men and does not allow for diversity: It suggests that because children are mostly reared by women in all societies, such a pattern should characterize all women and men. This explanation overlooks the fact that some men care for infants and enter caring professions, whereas not all women want to mother or do any other caring labor as adults. Moreover, it assumes that all children are being raised in a particular kind of family—a nuclear family consisting of a mother who is a sole and exclusive caretaker, a "breadwinner" father, and children. As the following chapters show, however, this type of family arrangement reflects the White middle-class heterosexual ideal of the family. Historically, parenting among the poor and in communities of color has rarely taken the form of **"intensive mothering"** implied by this theory. Poor and minority mothers, employed as low-wage labor, share the work of parenting with a variety of relatives and non-kin in the community (Collins 2000). Psychoanalytic theory, therefore, does a poor job of explaining gender differences in caregiving across race/ethnicity and class.

The second type of psychological explanation used to explain variation in family labor stresses "gender role **socialization**." In contrast to the psychoanalytic model, this theory focuses on conscious learning and modeling and argues that differences in ideologies, identities, and personalities are taught to women and men in early childhood. Collaborating with schools, peers, and the media, parents reward their sons and daughters for engaging in gender appropriate behavior. Children learn that certain types of labor are appropriate for men and for women, and they acquire personality traits and identities necessary to carry out these gender-specific tasks. Boys, for example, learn to be competitive and independent whereas girls learn to be nurturing and invested in personal relationships. These internalized ideas of gender-appropriate roles, identities, and personality traits, seen as rigid and unchanging after those early socialization years, govern people's choices in adult lives and explain the gendered division of labor.

In recent years, however, many scholars have critiqued this theory's assumption that personality traits and identities persist from early childhood into adulthood. In many ways, adult men and women take pathways very different from those they learned in childhood. And little research has been able to show that gendered ideologies can be traced back to early childhood.

Structure

Sociologists are more likely to focus on either **structure** or **culture** in adulthood when explaining gender differences in family labor. Structural explanations emphasize material constraints and opportunities embedded in employment experiences of women and men. Because men are more likely to be employed and, when employed, to have more lucrative as well as time consuming or satisfying jobs than women, their jobs pull or push them away from family responsibilities. According to this theory, when women have the same employment conditions as men, their caregiving will be the same as well.

Much literature on caregiving to parents has considered this explanation. Compared to employed women, the "traditional woman" who does not work for pay is especially likely to provide care to her relatives. Further, the types of help housewives and employed women give are different: Employed women continue to help, but especially with the kinds of tasks that consume not so much time as economic resources. They give more money and gifts while housewives do more time-consuming, hands-on chores.

Comparing employed women and employed men, we find that the gender difference in caregiving is reduced, primarily because having a job reduces the time daughters spend providing care, although that reduction appears to be offset by the employed daughters' substitution of financial for direct personal help (Gerstel and Gallagher 1994). When men and women retire, gender difference in caregiving decline: Retired men give more care, especially to their adult children, than employed men (Kahn, McGill, and Bianchi 2011).

Furthermore, even though by itself employment only accounts for a portion of the gender gap, job characteristics may help explain the rest: When men and women earn the same amount and are both self-employed, they give their parents the same amount of help (Sarkisian and Gerstel 2004a). As structural explanations would suggest, then, employed women look a lot like employed men (Gerstel 2000). Thus, it is not that men and women are biologically different, or that they were taught as children to behave in different ways. It is because adult women and men have different kinds of jobs that they give different amounts of care.

Another piece of evidence in support of this explanation comes from studies of gay and lesbian families. This scholarship finds that, just like heterosexual couples, gay and lesbian couples typically engage in a non-egalitarian division of carework and kinkeeping labor, and that this inequality is primarily driven by material conditions, especially the employment experiences of the partners (Carrington 1999).

Culture

The final explanation of gender differences in carework traces them to *culture* (West and Zimmerman 1987). As Swidler (2001) argues in her much cited work, culture is a repertoire or "tool kit" of habits, skills, and symbols that people use to construct life strategies. When faced, for example, with a relative who needs help, women are more likely than men to reach into their tool kit and decide that they should give care to that relative. As a result of that, their employment may suffer: Some women postpone entry into the labor force, limit their work hours, take time off, and even quit so they can do carework. In contrast, men's tool kit, according to this view, is much less likely to evoke this caregiving response; they neither view themselves nor other men as caregivers. Instead, men's cultural tool kit involves a view that people should be self-reliant and that caregiving is women's work.

Women and men have history on their side in this response: Family support systems have for over a century relied on the labor of women who think of themselves, and other women, as those who know how to, want to, and should give care to kin. And they have today's meaning systems on their side: Giving care entails the symbolic action of "**doing gender**" (West and Zimmerman 1987). Over the life course (not only in early childhood as argued by psychological theories), women and men adjust their expectations and pay attention to what others expect—to the cultural messages they receive from relatives and friends as well as from various institutions, especially churches and workplaces. While women meet the expectations of others by doing carework, men experience pressure to "do masculinity" by staying away from carework (Greenstein 2000).

In contrast to the structural theory, the cultural theory asserts that even when adult men and women are located in the same structural positions (e.g., hold the same jobs), they differ in the family work they do. For example, a married woman's decision about whether to be the primary breadwinner or work part-time to give care to a frail mother may depend on her own internalized beliefs about gender as well as beliefs of those around her—her husband, her siblings, her friends, and her mother.

Unfortunately, very few studies attempt to directly measure culture—usually, whatever is not explained by structural variables, researchers attribute to culture. And some studies do show that employed men do significantly less kin work than employed women, even if their employment conditions are similar (Gerstel and Gallagher 1994). Moreover, lacking direct measures of culture, some scholars (e.g., Brines 1994; Greenstein 2000) argue that ideas about "doing gender" can explain such gender differences. They propose, for example, that the reason employed married men do more housework than unemployed married men is because those without jobs have a greater need to demonstrate their masculinity to others and do so by avoiding family work. But without direct measurement of specific cultural influences, it remains unclear whether this avoidance can be attributed to men's own gendered beliefs or to their relatives' and friends' expectations. Overall, although culture likely shapes gender differences in paid and unpaid work, a growing number of theorists are "reluctant to divide culture and structure" (Small, Harding, and Lamont 2010: 8) because of the conceptual and methodological difficulties of fully disentangling them.

Conclusion

Historically and still today, women have served as the glue for extended families and community ties. If the structural theory of gender differences is correct, the gender gap should be changing as more and more women are employed in similar jobs as men. Thus, married women's increased entrance into "men's jobs" might sever the "kin work" that has organized and sustained what remains of the modern extended family. Alternatively, it is possible that kin work can be restructured, with men pitching in at higher rates.

To the extent that psychological differences or cultural processes are responsible, however, the gender gap will likely be more persistent. Although culture also shifts in tandem with structure, cultural changes tend to lag behind economic shifts. Moreover, men's and women's cultures might be changing at a different rate—Hochschild (1997) termed this phenomenon "the stalled gender revolution." For that reason, both sociologists and media pay a lot of attention to any signs of changes in men's attitudes and behaviors with regard to carework.

Some evidence suggests that such attitudes and behaviors have changed; however, some beliefs remain firmly gendered. Sociologist Kathleen Gerson, in her book *The Unfinished Revolution* (2010), finds that men and women still hold different expectations regarding their future work/family strategies. Neither young women nor young men want traditional families—regardless of the type of family in which they grew up. Both say they want egalitarian relationships in which they both do family work and both have independence and jobs. But they also have fall-back positions, which, Gerson suggests, create a new gender divide. Desiring autonomy, young women want both a career and an egalitarian relationship in which the couple shares caregiving, but if they cannot have both, they prefer to be independent and have a career. Young men also want egalitarian relationships, but when pressed, they speak of selecting a different fall-back strategy, where their careers come first while their wives provide most caregiving, even if that "choice" comes at the expense of the wives' careers. There is, then, an unfinished revolution, where the so-called "choices" of young men and women may collide.

DISCUSSION QUESTIONS

1. Think about a recent family celebration that included extended family members (for example, Thanksgiving, Chanukah, a wedding, a funeral, etc.). What kind of work went into getting the family together and making sure the celebration goes as planned? Who performed this work: Women, men, mothers, fathers, grandparents, aunts, uncles, or other relatives? Do your observations show that women are the glue holding your extended family together? Why or why not?
2. Why do people often not recognize caregiving and kinkeeping as work?
3. What are the main theories used to explain gender differences in care to extended families? Which of these explanations do you find the most compelling?

III: Race and Family Organization

I n his article titled "Why Our Black Families Are Failing" in *The Washington Post*, Raspberry (2005) declared: "What is happening to the black family in America is the sociological equivalent of global warming: easier to document than to reverse, inconsistent in its near-term effect—and disastrous in the long run." Such statements resonate with frequent media images of Black "welfare queens," deadbeat dads, neglected children, and teenage "baby mamas." While Raspberry's confident declaration expresses certainty that Black family life is in shambles, sociological literature on race/ethnicity and families is filled with disagreements, starting with a disagreement on who is actually more involved and engaged with their families—Whites, Blacks, or Latinos/as. This disagreement is closely related to family definitions and assumptions about families: Those who focus on marriage and nuclear families and those who examine extended families usually come to quite different conclusions.

Asian American families, Native American families, as well as families of other racial/ethnic groups are rarely mentioned in these debates. Unfortunately, there is little research on them, in part because there are fewer of them in the United States, and therefore national datasets contain too few cases to allow examination of their families. The focus on Blacks and Latinos/as is also politically driven. Politicians discuss the Black family in particular at length. Many have blamed the Black family for poverty, crime, and all sorts of social ills plaguing Black communities; oftentimes that argument has been used to justify the view of Blacks as undeserving of governmental aid. Recently, Latino/a families are also becoming a target for such debates as Latinos/as are now the largest racial/ethnic minority group in the United States.

A Little History: Disorganization of Black and Latino/a Families

Arguments about families of color have been the topic of longstanding and well-worn political debates. Making what we refer to as the "disorganization" argument, politicians often insist that Black and Latino/a families are both disorganized. One of the most prominent people making this argument was Daniel Patrick Moynihan, a White politician who was Assistant Secretary of Labor at the time he ignited the discussion on Black families and later became an influential U.S. Senator. His oft cited 1965 report for the Office of Policy Planning and Research of the U.S. Department of

Labor, titled *The Negro Family: A Case for National Action*, set the agenda and terms of the debate concerning Black families for many years.

Moynihan described the Black community as a "tangle of pathology" with high rates of unemployment and crime as well as illegitimacy, marital instability, and female-headed households. The family was not the victim, he argued, but instead the cause of the many social ills or "pathologies" concentrated in Black ghettoes. In the introduction to his report, Moynihan argued:

> The gap between the Negro and most other groups in American society is widening. The fundamental problem, in which this is most clearly the case, is that of family structure. The evidence—not final, but powerfully persuasive—is that the Negro family in the urban ghettos is crumbling. A middle-class group has managed to save itself, but for vast numbers of the unskilled, poorly educated city working class the fabric of conventional social relationships has all but disintegrated.

The problem, he suggested, was that,

> in essence, the Negro community has been forced into a **matriarchal** structure which, because it is too out of line with the rest of the American society, seriously retards the progress of the group as a whole, and imposes a crushing burden on the Negro male and, in consequence, on a great many Negro women as well."
>
> (Moynihan 1965: 29)

Later, he continued:

> at the center of the tangle of pathology is the weakness of the family structure. Once or twice removed, it will be found to be the principal source of most of the aberrant, inadequate, or antisocial behavior that did not establish, but now serves to perpetuate the cycle of poverty and deprivation. (30)

To be sure, Moynihan's ideas were not new, but he greatly contributed to popularizing this view. The pioneer of this approach was probably E. Franklin Frazier (1932), an eminent Black scholar who claimed that the conditions of slavery and the turmoil of emancipation disrupted Black nuclear families and eroded the cultural bases for "normal" family relations that might have existed in their African past. This view of history was later overturned by historian Herbert Gutman (1976) who showed that enslaved Blacks placed enormous value on their ties to spouses and children, and as a result, post-slavery, expended tremendous amounts of energy and money, even when they had very little of it, on the search for their spouses and children sold away during slavery. Gutman, nevertheless, also argued that Black families are disorganized, but he claimed it was because of migration to cities where racial discrimination undermined their ability to maintain family ties.

Even though decades have passed since Moynihan's report, many assumptions of the disorganization approach still dominate media and popular discourse on Black families and reappear in academic circles (e.g., Haskins 2009). Like Moynihan, most who take this approach now contend that Black families are disorganized, as indicated by high rates of out-of-wedlock births, sexual promiscuity, marital instability, and matriarchal families characterized by "strong and domineering" Black women who prefer to head families on their own. According to this view, these strong women push men away and raise emasculated sons unable to create a "normal" **patriarchal** nuclear family.

The story told about Latino/a families is more ambiguous, based on a somewhat different understanding and politics of gender. To be sure, some do argue that Latinas, in their role as single mothers, are the prime cause of a plethora of social ills in Latino/a communities. These scholars pathologize Latino/a families by arguing that Latinos/as, especially Puerto Ricans, have higher rates of out-of-wedlock births and single parenthood, which are responsible for their poverty and criminal engagement. Anthropologist Oscar Lewis, one of the pioneers of that argument, in his book, *La Vida: A Puerto Rican Family in the Culture of Poverty* (1965), detailed the life of one multi-generational Puerto Rican family living in La Perla, the most notorious slum of San Juan, Puerto Rico. He used his analysis of this family to argue that one of the main causes of Puerto Rican poverty was the *female*-headed household.

Other pathology narratives have been used for Latino/a families as well. One focuses on Latino/a cultural ideals of masculinity and femininity—*machismo* and *marianismo*—and suggests that they create unhealthy nuclear family dynamics. According to this argument, the main culprit in the Latino/a family "tangle of pathology" is the "macho" male: Driven by an inferiority complex and a rejection of authority, he tends to be overly aggressive, insensitive, unpredictable, invulnerable, and emotionally distant from his family—see review in Mirandé (1997). The cultural ideals of machismo are accompanied by a corresponding set of norms for women—marianismo. Based on the image of Virgin Mary, marianismo emphasizes passivity, docility, modesty, piety, sexual purity, and self-sacrifice as women's main virtues. This argument proposes that such a rigid cult of dominant masculinity and submissive femininity is the outgrowth of a unique cultural heritage that can be traced either to indigenous cultures such as Aztec or Taino or to the history of Spanish colonial rule in Latin America. These rigid gender norms create a dysfunctional hyper-authoritarian family whose members are unable to successfully navigate life in modern society. Unlike matriarchy arguments that have been directed more at Puerto Ricans than other Latinos/as, this approach emphasizes similarities across Latino/a groups.

Despite their differences, both these narratives of Latino/a family pathology, like the talk of Black family pathology, have focused on nuclear families. For Latinos/as, however, one additional "pathology" argument emerged that focuses instead on extended families: Some scholars pathologize Latino/a cultural preference for "clannishness"— extreme **familism**, a preoccupation with the family instead of the individual—that they assert characterizes high levels of attachment to extended families (see Baca Zinn and Wells 2000 for a review). According to this view, Latino/a "clannish" families impede assimilation and upward mobility in U.S. society.

The variety of pathology arguments concerning Latino/a families demonstrates that a social disorganization model makes it possible to declare pathological almost any family feature that distinguishes minority families from White families. For nuclear families, either a male-headed household is pathological because there is a "macho" man or a female-headed household is pathological because there is no man. Extended families, in turn, are afflicted by "pathology" either because they are "clannish" and therefore a detriment to Latino/a upward mobility, or because they entail a level of disorganization that makes it difficult to provide for their members' needs. Female or male-headed, clannish or disorganized, the Latino/a family is blamed for Latinos/as misfortunes (Baca Zinn and Wells 2000).

In sum, disorganization arguments about both Blacks and Latinos/as entail a set of assumptions about families of color—both what they are and what they should be. But what do the data show us about racial/ethnic differences in marriage and nuclear families?

Race, Marriage, and Nuclear Families: What Do the Data Show?

Research on racial/ethnic differences in marriage and childbearing confirms that Blacks and Latinos/as have lower rates of marriage as well as higher rates of single motherhood than non-Hispanic Whites. A recent comprehensive report issued by Pew Research Center (2010a) clearly demonstrates these differences. As Figure 3.1 shows,

Figure 3.1 Percent married by race and ethnicity, 1960–2008.

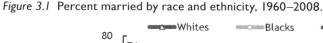

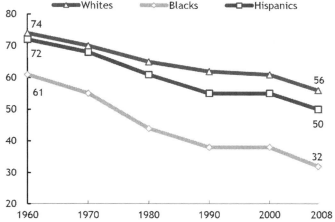

Note: Ages 18 and older. Hispanics are of any race. Whites and Blacks include only non-Hispanics.
Source: Pew Research Center (2010a) report, "The Decline of Marriage and Rise of New Families." Available from: http://pewsocialtrends.org/files/2010/11/pew-social-trends-2010-families.pdf. Based on Pew Research Center calculations using Decennial Census and American Community Survey data.

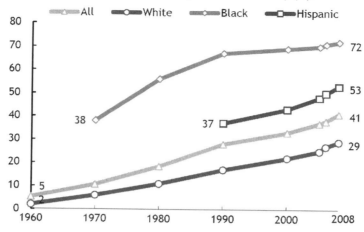

Figure 3.2 Share of births to unmarried women, by race and ethnicity (%).

Note: 2008 data are preliminary. Hispanics are of any race. Whites and Blacks include only non-Hispanics.
Source: Pew Research Center (2010a) report, "The Decline of Marriage and Rise of New Families." Available from: http://pewsocialtrends.org/files/2010/11/pew-social-trends-2010-families.pdf. For data from 1990 and later, statistics calculated using National Center for Health Statistics data. For years prior to 1990, data obtained from Ventura, Stephanie J., and Christine A. Bachrach. Nonmarital childbearing in the United States, 1940–1999. National Vital Statistics Reports; vol 48 no 16. Hyattsville, Maryland: National Center for Health Statistics.

the proportion of the population currently married has declined dramatically for all groups over the past 50 years, but the gap between Whites and Blacks has widened: Only 32 percent of Black adults are married, compared to 56 percent of Whites and 50 percent of Latinos/as.

Similarly, as Figure 3.2 shows, the share of births to unmarried women has increased dramatically over the same time period. Here, too, the gap between Blacks and Whites has widened: 72 percent of Black women giving birth are unmarried, compared to 53 percent of Latinas and 29 percent of White women.

Finally, Figure 3.3 presents data on the percentage of children living with a parent who has never been married. This rate has also risen dramatically over the same time period. In 1960, children of any race/ethnicity rarely resided with a never married parent: Less than 1 percent of White children, 1 percent of Latino/a children, and 2 percent of Black children lived in this type of household. That proportion has now reached 7 percent among White children, 18 percent among Latino/a children, and 41 percent among Black children.

But are these children of single parents—as they often appear in reports from the media and social commentators? Many of those who have children outside of marriage reside with a partner, at least when they give birth. As the Fragile Families and Child Wellbeing study demonstrates, more than half of children born outside of marriage reside with their fathers as well as mothers at the time of their first birthday. Even though that number declines to 35 percent by the children's fifth birthday, this still rep-

Figure 3.3 Share of children with a never married parent, by race and ethnicity (%).

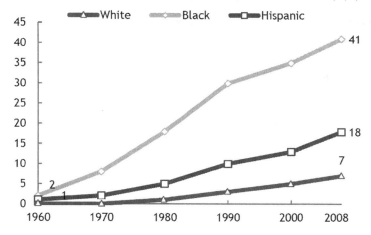

Note: Based on persons ages 17 and younger. Hispanics are of any race. Whites and Blacks include only non-Hispanics.
Source: Pew Research Center (2010a) report, "The Decline of Marriage and Rise of New Families." Available from: http://pewsocialtrends.org/files/2010/11/pew-social-trends-2010-families.pdf. Based on Pew Research Center calculations using Decennial Census and American Community Survey data.

resents a substantial share of two-parent households that are missed if we solely focus on marriage. Besides, Black and Mexican American cohabiting parents are less likely to break up than White cohabiting parents (Osborne, Manning, and Smock 2007).

Latinos/as are slightly less likely to be married than Whites, but they are not a homogenous population. As Figure 3.4 shows, Mexicans or Cubans have marriage

Figure 3.4 Percent currently married, by Latino/a subgroup.

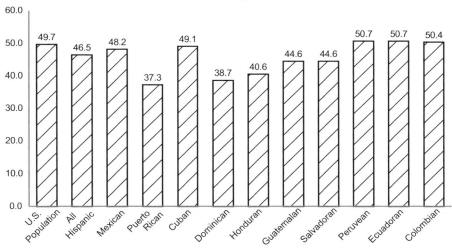

Note: Based on persons ages 15 and older.
Source: Pew Research Center (2010d) fact sheets, "Pew Hispanic Center Country of Origin Profiles, 2008." Available from: http://pewhispanic.org/data/origins. Based on Pew Research Center calculations using the Census Bureau's 2008 American Community Survey data.

Figure 3.5 Share of births to unmarried women, by Latina subgroup.

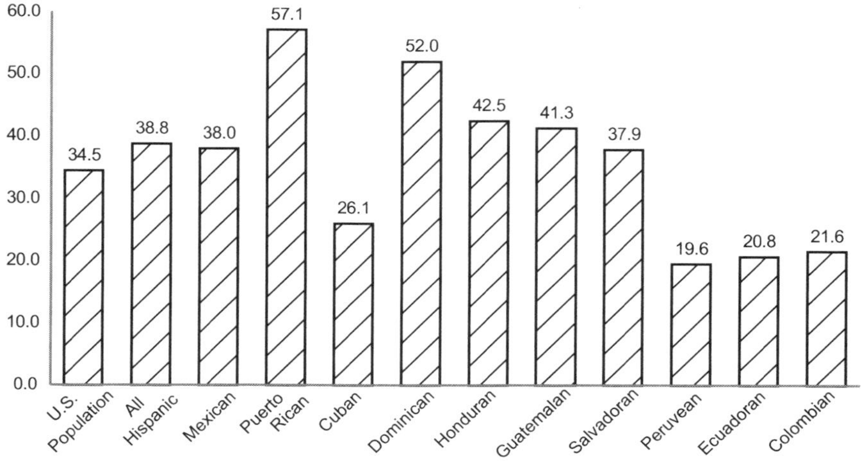

Bar chart values:
U.S. Population: 34.5
All Hispanic: 38.8
Mexican: 38.0
Puerto Rican: 57.1
Cuban: 26.1
Dominican: 52.0
Honduran: 42.5
Guatemalan: 41.3
Salvadoran: 37.9
Peruvean: 19.6
Ecuadoran: 20.8
Colombian: 21.6

Note: Women ages 15 to 44 who gave birth in the past 12 months.
Source: Pew Research Center (2010d) fact sheets, "Pew Hispanic Center Country of Origin Profiles, 2008." Available from: http://pewhispanic.org/data/origins. Based on Pew Research Center calculations using the Census Bureau's 2008 American Community Survey data.

rates similar to those of the U.S. population overall (49.7 percent), while other groups, such as Puerto Ricans and Dominicans, have substantially lower rates of marriage (37.3 percent and 38.7 percent, respectively). Similarly, as Figure 3.5 demonstrates, the rates of non-marital childbirth is also much higher among Puerto Ricans (57.1 percent) and Dominicans (52 percent) than in the general U.S. population (34.5 percent), while the prevalence of non-marital childbirth among Cubans is lower (26.1 percent).

Overall, these numbers demonstrate pronounced differences in the prevalence of "traditional" nuclear families between Whites and Blacks, and quite substantial differences between Whites and Puerto Ricans or Dominicans. These differences in marriage and parenting are often used as the empirical basis for claims that Black and Latino/a families are more disorganized than White families. But there is another side to the debate about race and families.

An Alternative Approach: The "Superorganization" of Families of Color

Since the Moynihan report, a number of criticisms have been directed at the "disorganization approach." Some criticized it for ignoring the contemporary oppression of Blacks, especially the multiple levels of oppression that Black women experience; others criticize it for blaming the family for the social ills found in communities of color. Critics also challenge the assumption that patriarchal nuclear family should be the norm and question whether the so-called "intact" nuclear family is always the best structure for adults and children. They point to negative effects of family conflict, often apparent in "intact" families, on both children and adults. Critics also point out that the disorganization focus on couples and children, or the "intact" nuclear family, implicitly assumes that reliance on relatives is a sign of familial dysfunction. Making what we call a "superorganization" argument, these critics suggests that Blacks and Latinos/as actually have better organized families than Whites, not only because of the processes within their nuclear families but also because of important ties among their extended families.

With regard to nuclear families, these scholars have noted that Black marriages are more likely to be egalitarian in their division of domestic labor (Collins 2000) and in terms of commitment to paid work. Bart Landry (2002) argues that Black middle-class couples forged a view of womanhood that combined a commitment to marriage with a commitment to paid jobs and community activities. The Black middle class, he suggests, pioneered the dual earner families that Whites later came to imitate. Similarly, Collins (2000) argued that for Black mothers, breadwinning is a central component of motherhood, and Damaske (2011) argues such job commitment still characterizes both working-class and middle-class Black women. Rare media accounts of work/family balance in Black families provide additional support: A *New York Times* article "Work vs. Family, Complicated by Race" (Clemetson 2006) refers to the Opt Out debates discussed in the previous chapter and argues that the "Mommy Wars" between employed mothers and stay-at-home mothers are less of an issue in Black communities, noting:

> For professional black women, debates about self-fulfillment can seem incomprehensibly narrow against the need to build sustainable wealth and security for their families. The discussions also pale in comparison to worries about shielding sons and daughters from the perils that black children face growing up, and overlook the practical pull of extended families in need of financial support.

With regard to Latino/a nuclear families, superorganization proponents argue that the concept of machismo should be seen in terms of Latino/a family pride and respect rather than male dominance (Mirandé 1997). They argue that machismo "includes the elements of courage, honor, and respect for others, as well as the notion of providing fully for one's family and maintaining close ties with the extended family" (Alvirez and Bean 1976: 278).

Those suggesting that Black and Latino/a families are better organized and more integrated acknowledge the higher prevalence of single mother households among Blacks and Puerto Ricans, but do not view these in a negative light. They repudiate the labels "intact" (to refer to nuclear families) and "broken" (to refer to non-nuclear families), arguing this linguistic distinction implies non-nuclear families are damaged. Instead, these superorganization theorists argue that Black and Latino/a families are not only better organized than White families but better equipped for the hardships of minority life. They positively interpret the strength of Black women as a characteristic that helps them persevere despite all odds. They also emphasize that Black non-resident fathers have higher levels of engagement with their children than White non-resident fathers (Edin, Tach, and Mincy 2009).

But at the heart of their critique is the importance of extended families in communities of color. Arguing that the focus on nuclear families characteristic of the disorganization approach is based on a White middle-class family model, critics point to the prevalence of extended kin networks among both Blacks and Latinos/as. Initially, these arguments emerged from ethnographic studies of Black and Latino/a communities. The most well known is Carol Stack's book *All Our Kin* (1974). In this ethnography of the poorest section of a Black community in a Midwestern city, Stack documented the extensive networks of exchanges among extended kin and fictive kin across and within households. Focusing on Latinos/as, ethnographies have also emphasized the high prevalence of extended family ties and the familistic attitudes of Latinos/as: For example, Rogler and Santana Cooney write:

> *Familism is* a traditional modality in Puerto Rico culture … The value system of familism, in its broadest terms, emphasizes the almost sacred bonds between relatives, the compelling obligations toward relatives, the duty to help and to express concern for them.
>
> (1984: 74)

A more recent study by Katherine Newman (1999) focused on working-poor Blacks and Latinos/as residing in Harlem and showed that even though poverty and crime continue to damage these communities, kinship networks and exchanges of support persist.

Most of these ethnographies stressed the central place that women occupy in these extended networks through their roles as mothers and "**othermothers**"—grandmothers, other female relatives, and non-relatives participating in a system of communal childrearing. They especially emphasize the importance of **reciprocity**—circular and balanced exchanges of help and support that take place in extended families of color.

Men are frequently portrayed as playing a more limited role in familial networks. For example, Stack, emphasizing that poor Blacks' networks of support were woman-centered, described the existence of social controls against the formation of marriages that could endanger the network of kin or the domestic authority of women. These controls, according to Stack, limited the roles of husbands or boyfriends within women's family networks. And a recent study of Black teen fathers (Paschal 2006) found that the main way many of these young men could contribute financially to their children was by relying on their female extended family—mothers, aunts, and grandmothers—who provided the kids of these teen dads with much needed economic support.

The emphasis on woman-centered networks is especially prominent in the literature on Blacks; for Latinos/as, there seems to be more of a gender balance. A recent study

(Haxton and Harknett 2009) showed Black parents emphasizing relations with female relatives and receiving support primarily from grandmothers of their children, while Latinos/as emphasized support from both grandparents.

Moreover, recently some superorganization scholars emphasized the role of men as well, arguing that Black men oftentimes contribute to multiple households simultaneously (e.g., those of their mothers, ex-wives, and girlfriends raising their children). Some black men also function as "other fathers"—uncles, other family members, or community members deeply involved in parenting children other than their own (Lempert 1999). In other words, rather than being disengaged from family life, Black men are often involved with several extended families.

These positive visions of families of color have brought a new round of criticism—with some disorganization scholars accepting the value of extended families but challenging their high prevalence among Blacks and Latinos/as. They argue that supportive extended kin networks among Blacks and Latinos have been destroyed by recent economic or cultural changes (e.g., Roschelle 1997; Patterson 1998). For example, Orlando Patterson in his book *Rituals of Blood* writes:

> As a result of their gender and familial problems, Afro-Americans are isolated not only from other Americans but from each other. Ironically, just the opposite stereotype about themselves prevails among Afro-Americans, in what I have called the myth of the "hood": the popular misconception that Afro-Americans compensate for their unmarried state by a higher involvement with their kinsmen and their communities.
>
> (1998: 161–162)

Some contemporary ethnographies corroborate his claims: One study of inner-city Black teenage mothers found that extended families were overstretched and even frequently hindered teenage moms (Kaplan 1997). Similarly, another study (McDonald and Armstrong 2001) suggested Black women in midlife are often not up to the task of supporting young mothers and argued that governmental policies and "**underclass**" culture have undermined traditional Black intergenerational support. Others emphasize men's detachment from extended family ties and suggest they substitute street-corner networks for familial ones (Anderson 1990).

In sum, while most theorists now agree that strong extended kin ties signal high levels of family organization, they disagree on the prevalence of these ties among Blacks, Latinos/as and Whites. So what does the evidence show?

What Do the Data Show about Race and Extended Families?

Our research using national surveys shows that minority individuals are more likely to live in extended family homes than Whites and in many ways more likely to help

Figure 3.6 Extended kin involvement among men, by race/ethnicity (%).

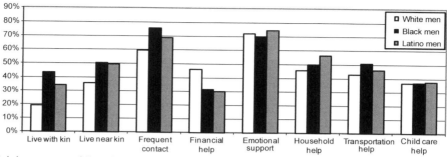

Note: Adult men ages 25 and older.
Source: Gerstel and Sarkisian (2008). Based on authors' calculations using National Survey of Families and Households data, 1992–1994.

out and rely on their relatives (Sarkisian and Gerstel 2004b; Sarkisian, Gerena, and Gerstel 2006, 2007; Sarkisian 2007; Gerstel and Sarkisian 2008). Figures 3.6 and 3.7 highlight some of the differences, separately for women and men. Looking at co-residence, approximately 40 percent of adult Blacks and about a third of Latinos/as—compared to under a fifth of Whites—share households with relatives. Similar patterns exist for living near relatives: Over half of Blacks and Latinos/as compared to only about a third of Whites live within two miles of kin. Blacks and Latinos/as are also more likely than Whites to visit relatives frequently.

Even if they don't live together, Blacks and Latinos/as are also more likely to rely on their relatives. However, there are important differences in the type of support. Whites are more likely than Blacks and Latinos/as to give and receive large sums of money. White women are more likely than minority women to give and receive emotional support—discuss personal problems, give each other advice. When it comes to practical tasks, however, we find that Black and Latino/a relatives are more likely than Whites to be supportive: They are more likely to give and receive help with household work and childcare, as well as provide rides and run errands.

Figure 3.7 Extended kin involvement among women, by race/ethnicity (%).

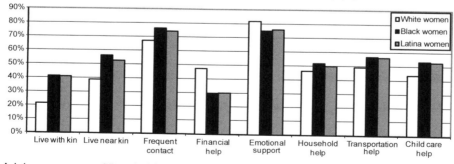

Note: Adult women ages 25 and older.
Source: Gerstel and Sarkisian (2008). Based on authors' calculations using National Survey of Families and Households, 1992–1994.

Interestingly, these ethnic differences in practical help are especially pronounced among women: Black women and Latinas are especially likely to participate in help exchanges. Black and Latino men are also involved with relatives, in contrast to pervasive images of minority men hanging out on street corners rather than attending to family ties. As Figure 3.6 shows, Black men and Latinos are more likely than White men to live near relatives and to stay in touch with them, although White men are more likely to give and receive large-scale financial support. The three groups of men are very similar, however, when it comes to practical help and emotional support.

In sum, there is not much support for disorganization theorists who argue that Blacks and Latinos/as have fewer extended kin ties than Whites. Even if some decline in extended family involvement among Blacks and Latinos/as has occurred, it did not make Blacks and Latinos/as less involved with extended families than Whites. Moreover, the little research that makes comparisons over time casts further doubt on the deterioration claim as it shows no drastic changes in family integration among Blacks (Taylor, Chatters, and Jackson 1997).

Conclusion

Minority families are disorganized only insofar as what we mean by family is limited to the nuclear family structure—as soon as we consider processes that occur within the nuclear family and examine extended family connections, a different picture emerges.

Once we recognize the importance of extended families among minorities, we should be careful not to overstate what they can accomplish. Even though Blacks and Latinos/as exchange more hands-on help with their relatives, that doesn't mean they get all the help they need. Greater support from relatives (who are often equally needy) usually cannot compensate for the disadvantages of being poor, or minority, or both. Thus, the relative levels of family support should not determine who gets assistance from the government—rather, we have to consider the overall level of need. In the next chapter, therefore, we will explore the link between economic circumstances and nuclear and extended family ties.

DISCUSSION QUESTIONS

1. What are the various ways in which the disorganization approach makes it possible to declare pathological almost any family feature that distinguishes minority families from White families?
2. How do superorganization scholars criticize the disorganization approach and what is their view of families of color?
3. What do the data show regarding the differences in nuclear and extended families among Whites, Blacks, and Latinos/as?

IV: The Power of Social Class

Structure, Culture, and Families as Strategies for Survival

This chapter turns to social class and considers how racial/ethnic differences in family experiences are tied to class differences. For most people, it comes as no surprise that class matters to family life. Movies like Trading Places and TV programs like *Wife Swap* and *The Simple Life* contrast the lifestyles of the rich and the poor, and family is certainly a large part of those lifestyles. Confirming this insight, a growing number of qualitative researchers who study families demonstrate the power of class. A number of these—including Lareau (2003), Edin and Kefalas (2007), and Edin, Tach, and Mincy (2009)—even argue, as we will argue in this chapter, that social class trumps race when it comes to families.

The surprise is not that class matters to family life but that class matters to the form family takes and how the family is constituted. As we will demonstrate, for the poor and near poor, family means extended family in a way it does not for the middle class or the rich. And it is these class differences—that is, differences in structural conditions—that are primarily responsible for the racial/ethnic variation in family life that we discussed in the previous chapter.

Attempting to explain race differences in family experiences, some scholars focus on cultural models while others emphasize structural patterns encountered by Blacks and Latinos/as vis-à-vis Whites. Interestingly, both those who emphasize culture and those who emphasize structure can be making either disorganization or superorganization arguments, creating four different positions represented in Table 4.1.

Two models rely on culture—the unique values and norms, beliefs and assumptions about family life shared by members of racial/ethnic groups. First, some have argued that families of color are culturally deficient. Second, others take the opposite position, arguing instead that families of color are resilient due to their cultural values. Both emphasize culture, but the former emphasizes problems of families of color while the latter emphasizes positive aspects. The same divide exists among those who rely on structure or the economic/material circumstances of racial/ethnic groups. Some emphasize structural destruction or problems of minority families while others take a structural resiliency approach and emphasize the positive aspects of the familial strategies in communities of color. We discuss and compare each of these four positions in turn.

Table 4.1 Explaining Difference: Families and Race

	Disorganized minority families	Superorganized minority families
Culture determines family organization	Cultural deficiency	Cultural resiliency
Structure determines family organization	Structural destruction	Structural resiliency

Note: For another version of this table, see Sarkisian and Gerstel (2004b).

1. Cultural Deficiency Approach

The first approach—"cultural deficiency"—stresses the purportedly deviant values, beliefs, and assumptions held by families of color. Those focusing on nuclear families were particularly likely to rely on this kind of explanation (e.g., Moynihan 1965; Patterson 1998). For Blacks, they especially emphasize the absence of norms promoting marriage, tolerance for nonmarital childbearing, preference for so-called "matriarchy," and general cynicism and lack of social trust. They trace the origins of these cultural values to slavery or the subsequent years of oppression, but argue that eventually these values took on a life of their own, transmitted from generation to generation in a self-perpetuating cycle of pathology. This cycle of pathology is frequently termed the "culture of poverty," a term coined by Oscar Lewis (1965) in his study of Puerto Rican families that we discussed in the previous chapter. Broadly, the culture of poverty argument suggests that poor people have cultural norms and values that are different from "mainstream" values and norms. These norms are traced to the material hardship and lack of economic opportunities among earlier generations, but once the culture of poverty has developed, the poor are unable to take advantage of economic opportunities even if they do become available—cultural "deviance" prevents the poor from moving up the socioeconomic ladder. That is, according to this approach, racism, discrimination, and oppression of racial/ethnic minorities are things of the past, while in the present, poverty and family "disorganization" stem mostly from choices based on deficient cultural values.

With regard to Latinos/as, cultural deficiency approaches blame the values of machismo and marianismo as well as the "over the top," "clannish" familism that purportedly prevents upward mobility. The assumption is that these values are prevalent in all Latin American countries, and that Latinos/as resist assimilation and preserve these after immigrating to the United States.

Abundant critiques directed at cultural deficiency approaches made them unpopular in academic circles for a while, even though conservative politicians and pundits continued to rely on such perspectives as they provide a convenient justification for not doing much to help the poor: After all, if the poor have deficient values, they are to blame for their own misfortunes. Recently, some scholars have reinvigorated the cultural deficiency perspective in academic literature as well. For example, Orlando

Patterson in his book *Rituals of Blood* (1998: 160) stated that "ex-slaves emerged after emancipation with chronic gender and familial problems," and argued:

> Let us be clear about what are not presently the causes of the problem: low income or joblessness among Afro-American men. ... *current* economic factors are no longer at the root of the problem. ... The cultural damage [was] already done, today these factors make no difference.
>
> (1998: 163)

Interestingly, while Patterson emphasizes that men are especially detached from families, he refrains from blaming this detachment on the cultural values of Black women, blaming it instead on the cultural values of men themselves.

Following in Patterson's footsteps, a recent issue of the ANNALS of the American Academy of Political and Social Science, titled "Reconsidering Culture and Poverty," *was dedicated specifically to the link between culture and poverty*. The volume was celebrated with a congressional briefing and received a warm welcome from the media. In her *New York Times* article, Patricia Cohen (2010) wrote: "For more than 40 years, social scientists investigating the causes of poverty have tended to treat cultural explanations like Lord Voldemort: That Which Must Not Be Named," and declared that "'Culture of Poverty' Makes a Comeback." Even though the editors and the authors tried to carefully distinguish themselves from the traditional "culture of poverty" approach and "rarely claim that culture will perpetuate itself for multiple generations regardless of structural changes" (Small, Harding, and Lamont 2010: 8), the volume reflects the same focus on the nuclear family and lack of attention to other forms of family ties.

2. Cultural Resiliency Approach

The second cultural approach—the "cultural resiliency approach"—focuses on positive aspects of Black and Latino/a families—strong mother-child relationships, communal patterns of childcare, and extended families—and argues that these result from adaptive cultural values of minorities. Some scholars making these arguments suggest that these distinctive cultural values—for Blacks in particular—are a result of the cultural legacy of slavery and years of oppression that generated a range of adaptive responses, boosting ethnic solidarity, extended familism (Aschenbrenner 1975), altruism (Stoll 2001), and religiosity (Musick, Wilson, and Bynum 2000).

Other proponents of the cultural resiliency approach argue that these are values rooted in Blacks' African heritage (Sudarkasa 1996) or a unique cultural heritage that can be traced either to Spanish colonial influences or to indigenous cultures such as Aztec or Taino (Fernandez Mendez 1993). They argue that preservation of African, indigenous, or traditional Spanish cultures manifested itself through extended familistic values, a high value placed on childrearing and motherhood, and, especially for Blacks, acceptance of nonmaternal care of children. As a result, they argue, contemporary Blacks and Latinos/as possess a strong family orientation and elaborate systems of kinship. For instance, addressing Black families, Sudarkasa wrote:

> … even though the constraints of slavery did prohibit the replication of African lineage ("clan") and family life in America, the principles on which these kin groups were based, and the values underlying them, led to the emergence of variants of African family life in the form of the extended families which developed among the enslaved Blacks in America.

> (1996: 29)

Some criticized this approach for locating all Black and Latino/a distinctiveness in the past (i.e., African or indigenous past, or slavery and colonialism), and therefore understating the effects of contemporary economic and social institutions on Black and Latino/a families (Roschelle 1997). Another problem is that it tends to romanticize the strength of minority women, neglecting the burdens that gender, class, and racial/ethnic oppression place on them (Collins 2000; Roschelle 1997). It glorifies "superorganized" families of color while underemphasizing the problems that they face.

3. Structural Destruction Approach

The third view—the "structural destruction approach"—focuses again on problems of families of color but argues that it is structural conditions, rather than values or beliefs, that are responsible for racial differences in families. Scholars holding this view argue that the intensive ties among relatives that used to characterize Black and Latino/a communities have been destroyed by recent economic and social changes. For example, Roschelle (1997: 184) wrote: "One could argue that current economic conditions have become so severe that they prevent minority families from participating in their social support networks because these families no longer have any resources to share." Similarly, Menjivar (1997, 2000) attributed Latinos/as' low levels of involvement with extended family to poverty and associated hardships of immigration. She wrote: "Extreme poverty and scarcity arising from a historically specific confluence of factors upset the flow of material assistance and hinder sharing among kin-related immigrants, effectively debasing these ties' potential for support" (1997: 120).

Structural destruction scholars argue that higher socioeconomic standing—higher income, better education—means more resources to share; these in turn boost family ties. Thus, they attribute the perceived decline in Black and Latino/a family ties to persistent and residentially concentrated poverty and increasing joblessness which undermine both nuclear and extended family ties. Some also trace minority family disruption to the troubles associated with poverty, such as drugs and crime (Anderson 1990). Finally, others argue that liberal social policy disrupted family networks through generous provision of financial help that substituted for extended family support (McDonald and Armstrong 2001). The structural destruction approach, however, has been criticized for its tendency to generalize "underclass" findings to all Blacks, neglecting the diversity among them.

4. Structural Resiliency Approach

The fourth and final approach—labeled "structural resiliency"—turns again to the positive aspects of families of color and emphasizes that Blacks' and Latinos/as' higher levels of involvement with extended families result from contemporary economic and social conditions. Specifically, proponents of the structural resiliency approach argue that poverty and oppression bring extended families closer together. Strong family ties and a high degree of reciprocal exchanges are a necessity, a strategy to ensure survival. The differences between White families and families of color result from their different contemporary structural positions, such as differences in education, income, and wealth, which translate into different levels of need for help and support. These theorists insist that to make ends meet, poor Blacks and Latinos/as need to maintain higher levels of familial involvement. Importantly, this approach views the need for social support as the primary mechanism producing such support. For instance, Carol Stack (1974) wrote that poor Black families:

> … share with one another because of the urgency of their needs. Alliances between individuals are created around the clock as kin and friends exchange and give and obligate one another. They trade food stamps, rent money, a TV, hats, dice, a car, a nickel here, a cigarette there, food, milk, grits, and children.
>
> (Stack 1974: 32)

Similarly, Katherine Newman (1999) emphasizes economic necessity as the primary driving force producing reliance on extended families among the Black and Latino/a families she observed. Newman explains:

> Public perceptions of America center around middle-class nuclear families as the norm, the goal toward which others should be striving. Yet in those suburban households, it would be rare to find the intensity of relations that knits these sisters and cousins together, keeping them in daily contact with one another. Middle-class Americans value autonomy, including autonomous relations between generations and siblings once they reach adulthood.
>
> (Newman 1999: 192–193)

She then emphasizes the power of structural constraints:

> And, of course, if they have a stable hold on a decent income, there is little forcing them together into the sort of private safety net that Latoya [an African American woman whom Newman interviewed] and her relatives maintain.

Newman also observes similar dynamics for Latinos/as, especially first-generation immigrants:

> Immigrants cluster into apartment buildings in much the same fashion as the African American poor do, both because relatives have been instrumental in helping their family members find housing and because proximity makes it that much easier to organize collective child-minding or communal meals.

Newman highlights the example of Carmen, a Dominican immigrant whose family she observed, to describe the intense kin ties she found:

> In Carmen's building there are five households linked together by kinship connections. Their members move freely between them, opening the refrigerator door in one to see whether there's anything good to eat, watching television in another because it has cable hookup, using the one phone that hasn't been cut off for nonpayment. Carmen's grandmother watches her grandchildren, a half-dozen in all now, so that their parents can go to work.

In sum, according to these structural approaches, Black and Latino/a families are different from White families primarily because they are more likely to be poor: Race yields little effect independent of socioeconomic position. Families that face similar material conditions will tend to have similar family organization.

Empirical Evidence on Race, Class, and Culture

Clearly, the empirical evidence on extended families among Blacks and Latinos/as that we presented in the previous chapter contradicts at least to some extent both the cultural deficiency and structural destruction approaches, as we reported that minority extended family members live closer to one another and are more likely to exchange help than White family members. So we cannot label them either deficient or destroyed. But that leaves the other two approaches: *Cultural resiliency*, which relies on culture to explain the differences, and *structural resiliency* that relies on structural patterns to explain the differences. Now we ask again: What does the research show?

In our own research using data from a large nationwide survey—the National Survey of Families and Households (Sarkisian and Gerstel 2004b; Sarkisian, Gerena, and Gerstel 2006, 2007), we found that social class rather than culture is the key to understanding the differences in extended family ties and behaviors between Whites and ethnic minorities.

To be sure, differences in cultural values do exist, but the patterns are not as straight-forward as either cultural deficiency or cultural resiliency theorists lead us to expect. Both Whites and Blacks are more likely than Latinos/as to agree that women and men can be fulfilled without marriage and that divorce in an unhappy marriage with a child under five is acceptable. Yet, Blacks and Latinos believe more strongly than Whites that it is generally better for the children if the couple stays together when a marriage is troubled. At the same time, all three racial groups equally believe that marriage should be for life. The latter finding, reflecting the continuing commitment to marriage across all groups in American society, accords with the recent Pew Research Center (2010a) report showing that unmarried Blacks are just as likely as unmarried Whites to say they would like to get married in the future.

That does not mean, however, that members of different racial/ethnic groups are unrealistic about their chances of getting and staying married. Blacks are more likely than Whites to agree that marriage is becoming obsolete (Pew Research Center 2010a), and Blacks and Latinos/as are more accepting of non-marital childbearing than Whites. Blacks are more likely than Whites to accept cohabitation for those planning to marry. Blacks tend to hold more egalitarian beliefs about gender than Whites, while Latinos/as, especially Mexican Americans, tend to hold more "traditional" views. Furthermore, Blacks and Latinos/as are more likely than Whites to think adult children and aging parents have obligations to care for one another (Sarkisian and Gerstel 2004b). However interesting these differences in values are, they explain only a small portion of the gap between Whites and racial/ethnic minorities in terms of their actual involvement with relatives. It is, instead, social class that matters most in explaining these differences.

It is widely known (and confirmed by Table 4.2) that Blacks and Latinos/as tend to have far less income and education than Whites. Families of color are also much more likely than White families to be below the official poverty line. These structural disadvantages certainly contribute to racial/ethnic differences in nuclear family structure:

Table 4.2 Education, Income, and Poverty Rates by Race/Ethnicity

	Whites	Blacks	Latinos/as
Median household income	$54,620	$32,068	$37,759
Percentage below poverty line	9.9%	27.4%	26.6%
Education:			
Not high school graduate	12.4%	15.8%	37.1%
High school graduate	57.3%	64.4%	49.0%
College graduate or more	30.3%	19.8%	13.9%

Sources: U.S. Census Bureau (2011b, 2011c).

As Pew Research Center (2010a) report puts it: "Marriage, while declining among all groups, remains the norm for adults with a college education and good income but is now markedly less prevalent among those on the lower rungs of the socio-economic ladder." In our research, we find that the differences in extended family ties between Whites and ethnic minorities are also primarily the result of these social class disparities.

Simply put, Whites, Blacks, and Latinos/as with the same amount of income and education have similar patterns of involvement with their extended families. More specifically, it is because Whites tend to have more income than Blacks and Latinos/as that they are more likely to give money to their relatives. And the higher levels of advice and emotional support found among White women can be at least in part traced to their higher levels of education, perhaps because schooling encourages women to talk out their problems.

Conversely, individuals' lack of economic resources increases their need for practical help from relatives and boosts their willingness to give help in return. Because Blacks and Latinos/as typically have less income and education than Whites, they come to rely more on their relatives for daily needs such as childcare, household tasks, or rides. Not only do they exchange this mutual aid, but, as we saw in the previous chapter, they are more likely to visit each other and live together. The tendency of Blacks and Latinos/as to live with or near relatives may also reflect their greater need for kin cooperation, as well as their decreased opportunities and pressures to move away, including moving for college.

As this analysis suggests, routine engagement with extended family members is largely a survival strategy in the face of economic difficulties. Blacks and Latinos/as are less likely to have the economic resources that allow the kind of privatization or separation that the nuclear family entails. That is, helping others with practical matters and getting help from them is a *class-based* strategy for survival. Class trumps race in this regard.

Rich Families, Poor Families

To further clarify the place of class in shaping reliance on extended families, we turn to some research that included intensive interviews with physicians and nursing assistants (Clawson, Gerstel, and Crocker 2009; Gerstel, Clawson, and Huyser 2007; Shows and Gerstel 2009). These are in some sense at the two ends of a class (and gender and race) continuum: Physicians, many of whom are married White men, earning an average yearly income of $160,000, and nursing assistants, many of whom are single mothers of color earning an average of $20,000 a year.

The researchers asked them to talk about their families (Gerstel 2011). The male physicians talked about their wives and children; they rarely talked about extended family. When they did, they talked most often about their aging parents and adult children; only one mentioned a brother. Moreover, they tended to talk about visits more than assistance. When they did talk about practical help, it usually took two forms. First, sometimes they talked about the help their parents or another relative gave them with childcare. But this is mostly a kind of supplementary care their parents provide on an occasional Saturday or Sunday—care that augments the often expensive childcare they purchase and the intensive mothering their wives provide. One physician first emphasized the importance of family, saying: "It's just nice having family around, to help out" and added that his wife's parents help with the kids. When asked how often, he responded:

> They're away during the winter time. They go to Florida. They go from November to April. So there's six months a year that they're away but there's the other six months. ... I'd say they take the kids every—once a week, once every two weeks.

Second, sometimes physicians talked about the other end of the life course—care for elderly parents. But this, too, they generally conceive of as a supplement to paid care. These upper middle-class physicians are not a population deeply immersed in extended families.

The low-wage nursing assistants tell a very different story. For them, extended families are central. Many talk about intense exchanges with their mothers and grandmothers and, less often, grandfathers; the older ones talk about their own grown daughters and sons. Many also talk about relationships with and assistance to and from siblings, cousins, aunts and uncles, nieces and nephews. To be sure, we should not romanticize these relationships with extended families; the nursing assistants occasionally complain or express ambivalence about these relationships. For example, one twenty-five year old single Latina mom who turns to her three sisters and mom for a great deal of help with her kids, said of them:

> They'll talk all this junk about doing it, because when they do something for me they complain, but that's how it goes with family.

But many also made comments like: "I don't know what I would do without my sister." Similarly, referring to her mother, another insisted: "She is my rock. She is my life." Sometimes nursing assistants live with extended family members—echoing the patterns of relatives sharing households that survey data show is so frequent among the less affluent. They talk about sharing their homes with young relatives, like nieces and nephews; they talk about living with older relatives—mothers, siblings, aunts—and giving one another reciprocal assistance. Listen to how filled with relatives their lives can be:

Well, I'm a single parent. That's my aunt (pointing to another person who worked in the same nursing home), so I stay with her. ... Usually if both of us have to work the same day, that guy that you just saw in here, that's my cousin, and that's his girlfriend. So if we all have to work, I'll stay here till 8:00 and bring the kids to their house, which is the next block over. Right, we all kind of work together to make it happen.

Much of the reason why these nursing assistants rely so much on relatives has to do with the kinds of jobs they have. Again, compare them to the physicians. To be sure, the physicians' jobs require long hours, and they often complain about the burden of those hours, but their hours are flexible: Many physicians can, and do, cancel appointments—sometimes because of more pressing work demands elsewhere but also to go on vacations, attend a professional meeting, or occasionally attend a child's ballet, soccer, or piano performance. They simply ask their scheduler not to plan or to cancel appointments when they want to do these other things. The nursing assistants have far less flexibility or control over their work hours. Moreover, although they do not work as many hours as the physicians (in fact, nursing assistants sometimes complain of the limits employers place on overtime because they need money), many work what have come to be known as "alternative schedules"—those shifts that occur during evenings and nights. Because of these odd hours, the nursing assistants need help, especially but not only with childcare. They turn to extended family, especially mothers and siblings. One nursing assistant—a single mother who works the evening shift—told this story about how she has to rely on kin:

> ... sometimes it's hard to find a babysitter from 3 to 11, 'cause people got lives, like my sister, she got two other kids, and it's hard so ... She just goes, picks him up in school, then she drops him off at my mom's house. That's what she does ... he sleeps with my mom ...

Another nursing aide emphasizes how the "alternative" hours required reliance on her extended family:

> And then on a weekend I'll ask one of my brothers if they could do baby-sitting for me; in the nursing field you *have* to—it's a *must*—you have to work every other weekend ... Right now I'm watching my nephew for my brother.

Clearly, extended kin *are* family for these low wage nursing assistants. This is best summed up by another nursing assistant, a 20 year old African American who lives with a male partner and a six year old son, who remarks: "I don't actually have family out here. My family's in Philly." For her, family is not her partner and son; family is her relatives—her mother, cousins, and grandparents.

Conclusion

In sum, for the poor and near poor, family means extended family in a way it does not for the middle class. As Matilda Riley (Riley and Riley 1993) argued some time ago, kinship connections form a "latent matrix"—that is, they can be and are activated at times of crisis or need. The poor and working class *often* encounter such needs, even crises—the latent matrix becomes, for them, a routine and very much manifest matrix of care. Although cultural values may influence the families, this chapter has shown that it is primarily the structural conditions that shape them.

While we can emphasize that research does not support the view that poor or minority families are disorganized, we should not romanticize extended family ties of the poor. Just as the poor rely on them, they sometimes point to tensions in those much needed relationships. Relations with relatives are not always harmonious nor are they simply based on altruism; instead they rest on need and a belief in reciprocity. Maureen Perry-Jenkins (2004) found that the low-wage new parents she studied, who often relied on relatives for childcare, were sometimes troubled by their sense of indebtedness and obligation to "pay back" service or care. Moreover, Stack (1974) found that the reciprocal patterns of sharing with relatives, forged in order to survive hardship, often made it difficult for poor Blacks to get married or escape poverty. This strategy for survival, then, has its own tensions and costs.

Some argue that the concentration of extended family support primarily among those with few resources might be changing as middle-class Americans increasingly rely on extended families. Karen Hansen in her book *Not-So-Nuclear Families* argues:

> As families across the economic spectrum search for alternative strategies to make child rearing and family life feasible, white middle-class families are restructuring kin relationships, following the path of African Americans, immigrants, and members of the working class.

> (2005: 4)

In partial support of that assertion, recent Census data (U.S. Census Bureau 2011) show that, while the number of children living with at least one grandparent has increased overall, that increase is much steeper among Whites. Although we might be tempted to romanticize these increases as a return to the "good old days," it is important to resist such urges: These changes are much more likely to result from a worsening economy than from increases in familistic values. Indeed, increases in reliance on extended families were particularly pronounced during the Great Recession (Cohen 2011; Pew Research Center 2010b).

There may be some other reasons for such increases as well. Vern Bengtson, who argued that "for many Americans, multigenerational bonds are becoming more important than nuclear family ties for well-being and support over the course of their life," cited reasons such as:

(a) the demographic changes of population aging, resulting in "longer years of shared lives" between generations; (b) the increasing importance of grandparents and other kin in fulfilling family functions; (c) the strength and resilience of intergenerational solidarity over time.

(Vern Bengtson 2001: 1)

He also argued that the decreased stability of marriages make extended kin ties more enduring and reliable than nuclear family ties. To address this issue, we will explore how marital ties and extended family relationships are connected in the next chapter.

DISCUSSION QUESTIONS

1. What are the two main explanations for racial/ethnic differences in family? How is each of them used to account for disorganization and superorganization arguments?
2. What does the research show regarding the explanations for racial/ethnic differences in extended family ties?
3. What do we mean when we say that class trumps race when it comes to explaining extended family patterns?

V: Marriage and Families

~~~~~~

Previous chapters show that a focus on marriage and the nuclear family misses a great deal of family life and denigrates poor families. In this chapter, we turn to the relationship of marriage to extended families and the community. We suggest that in many ways, marriage separates men and women from these social connections.

This view flies in the face of much popular press and political rhetoric. For many social critics and observers, not only is the nuclear family the basic unit of society, but marriage is the fundamental connective tissue in the community. Marriage, to them, is the endangered foundation of a healthy society, whose fragility threatens children and adults as well as the broader community. Welfare reformers, both Republicans and Democrats, emphasize marriage as a route out of poverty for single mothers and a route to responsibility for unmarried fathers. Recent administrations and Congress have redirected millions of dollars to marriage initiatives and incentives, workshops and classes intended to turn the tide back toward marriage. Likewise, many gay and lesbian groups place marriage at the center of their political agenda.

Many researchers quickly joined politicians in loud support of marriage, citing research showing that marriage is good for one's pocketbook, health, happiness, sex life, and kids. Married individuals tend to have higher income, more wealth, better health benefits, and more property than the unmarried. Married couples cozying up at home have sex more often than singles, whom we imagine partying until dawn. Then there are the physical and mental health benefits of marriage—especially for men but also for women. Marriage, or at least good marriages with little conflict, protects individuals from everything from cavities to murder and suicide. As Christakis and Fowler (2009: 86) write: "Being married adds seven years to a man's life and two years to a woman's life—better benefits than most medical treatments." Some further note that marriage keeps adult men out of crime and their kids out of delinquency. Many recent advocates insist that benefits of marriage accrue to both women and men.

Skeptics dismiss these benefits as "**self-selection effects**": It isn't marriage itself that has salutary effects but rather those who are healthier and wealthier, sexier and more law abiding are more likely to find and keep spouses. Men with higher earnings are more likely to marry. Those in trouble with the law are less likely to go to the altar. The sick and the poor are more likely to divorce. Proponents, however, insist that marriage itself creates most of these beneficial effects.

Just a few decades ago, however, feminists—heterosexual and lesbian alike—insisted on exposing some of the problems with marriage. Arlie Hochschild, a well-known sociologist, captured how things changed when she wrote in the *New York Times*:

> One June day in 1977, my husband and I and our two small children stood on a San Francisco street corner to watch the annual gay pride parade. Amid the balloons and streamers, we saw a sign bob by: "Smash the Nuclear Family." On the same street corner 32 years later, we saw another parade and a different sign: "YES on Gay Marriage!" As an ideal at least, American marriage has survived a cultural war unmatched in the Western world.

Some researchers today still identify the costs of marriage, especially for women. Women's housework increases (and men's decreases) after a couple heads down the aisle. All too many married women experience domestic violence—physical, sexual, emotional. Plus, marriage brings fewer benefits to the poor than the affluent. Sociologists Kathryn Edin and Maria Kefalas (2005) find that poor women have babies but do not get married because potential husbands would impose constraints and often cost rather than contribute money. And only marriages with low levels of conflict offer health benefits. In contrast, bad marriages are hazardous to mental and physical health, increasing suicide, stress, cancer, and blood pressure. Lots of marriages have conflict and hostility and many deteriorate over time. Still, this debate generally focuses "inward"—both proponents and critics discuss marriage's benefits and costs for the individual wife, husband, and children. This chapter moves outward, examining the consequences of marriage for ties to relatives and the broader community.

A few decades ago, some scholars of family and kinship suggested that modern marriage competes with, even undermines, relations in the wider community. Lewis and Rose Coser (1974) described marriage as a "greedy institution" demanding "undivided commitment." In their book *Anti-Social Family*, Michelle Barrett and Mary McIntosh (1982) went further, suggesting marriage was a "trap" or a "prison"—an exclusive relationship that harmed other relationships. What does empirical research show?

Extended Family Ties and Marriage

Our analyses of two nationwide surveys (Gerstel and Sarkisian 2006, 2007; Sarkisian and Gerstel 2008) show that married people—women as well as men—are less involved with extended families than the unmarried. As Figure 5.1 demonstrates, not surprisingly, married people are much less likely than singles to live with their parents or siblings. But the married are also less likely to visit relatives and give them less emotional support, advice, or practical help. Married adult children take care of elderly

Figure 5.1 Marital status and involvement with parents and siblings.

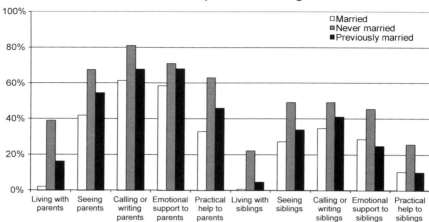

Source: Gerstel and Sarkisian (2006). Based on authors' calculations using National Survey of Families and Households, 1992–1994.

parents less often than their unmarried siblings. And, compared to those without a spouse, married adult children are less involved with their siblings.

Originally, the Cosers coined the phrase "marriage as a greedy institution" to discuss housewives who focused on the home. Therefore, we might expect a gender gap—that marriage would isolate women more than men. Our research, however, shows that marriage constricts both women's and men's social relationships. In some ways, the effects of marriage are greater for men than for women. For example, married women talk on the phone to their parents and siblings less often than those who never got married, or left or lost a husband. But the difference is more dramatic for men: Lots of husbands rely on wives to call their relatives while men without wives make the connection themselves. Moreover, marriage may reduce women's and men's ties for different reasons. Because men have greater marital power and preference for a single confidant (their wife), and women are socialized to connect to and take care of a range of family and friends, the diminution of wives' ties might result more from their husbands' needs and desires than from their own.

Marriage and Other Social Connections

What about other people in the community, like friends and neighbors? From *Full House* to *Sex in the City, Friends*, and *OC* to "reality shows" like *Laguna Beach* and *Jersey Shore*, television offers us images of singles who hang out with their coupled buddies. TV friendships outlast or at least coexist with romantic relationships, even marriage. Is this what real life is like? Not too often.

As Figure 5.2 illustrates, compared to those never or previously married, married couples are less likely to socialize with neighbors and friends. And those never married

Figure 5.2 Marital status and involvement with neighbors and friends.

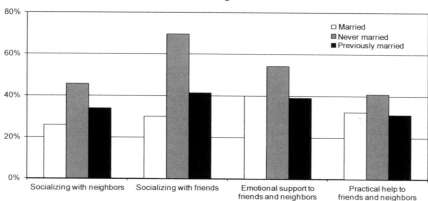

Source: Gerstel and Sarkisian (2006). Based on authors' calculations using General Social Survey, 2004 and National Survey of Families and Households, 1992–1994.

are more likely than the married to offer a hand or an ear—to give either emotional support or practical help. These patterns look the same for women and men. The differences appear especially large when those currently married are compared to the never married. The previously married, though still experiencing the effects of marriage, seem to be on the path of returning to their pre-marital levels of socializing. But because friends, like property, are often split when marriages end, it is difficult for the previously married to catch up to those who never got married.

To be sure, marriage intensifies some social connections, especially for men. Marriage increases people's volunteering, whether for religious, youth, or health and human services organizations. But married people volunteer more because of their higher levels of education and higher rates of parenthood rather than because of marriage itself. One type of volunteering remains more prominent among the married, especially married men, even if we take parenthood and education into account: The married are especially likely to volunteer for religious organizations. Why? Marriage and religion are likely linked in many ways: Religious individuals are more likely to marry; religious institutions legitimate marriage through rituals and programs as well as provide support—both social and normative—to married couples, who, in turn, volunteer for these religious organizations. For the most part, however, marriage constrains social connections.

These findings contradict some classical sociological accounts. For instance, the widely cited theorist Émile Durkheim (1966) maintained that marriage fostered investment in social ties. And Slater (1963), in his classic piece on dyadic withdrawal, argued that marriage and its rituals provide an institutional solution to a couple's natural inclination to withdraw from community networks. To be sure, weddings usually do involve extended families and communities, and many other rituals from funerals to baby showers, family reunions, or holidays such as Thanksgiving and Mother's Day, Father's Day, or Grandparents' Day involve married couples and might help couples reconnect with their relatives. Despite these rituals, we find that married couples are more isolated from extended families and broader social ties than single individuals.

Why Does Marriage Isolate?

Once again, there can be sociobiological, psychological, structural, and cultural explanations for these effects of marriage. Or these effects might stem from self-selection—that is, who it is that gets married.

Biology and Psychology

Both sociobiological and psychological explanations suggest there is a universal link between marriage and other social ties: They argue that marriage—and human coupling in general—demands a kind of intense involvement that necessarily detracts from other relationships and from activities that might draw the couple away from their shared home. Thus, these theories suggest the married are naturally and necessarily homebodies.

Such tendencies are most obvious with the newly connected couple, all wrapped up in one another with little interest in others. Many have experienced the kind of intense involvement in new relationships where ties to others pale by comparison; most have experienced the difficulty of being around such starry-eyed couples. But the short-circuiting of community ties characterizes not just oblivious "young" lovers but also longstanding married couples.

According to biological and psychological approaches, this process is universal across human societies. As we show below, this assumption is seriously flawed: The short-circuiting of community ties is not universal; it reflects the isolationist character of marriage in the contemporary United States.

Structure

The second set of explanations—structural—suggest that differences between the married and the unmarried stem not from the invariant nature of human coupling but from differences in resources, opportunities, and constraints. In the contemporary United States, married people are better educated and more likely to have well-paying careers than the unmarried. So maybe it is those time-consuming well-paid jobs that cut off relationships. Or, in light of previous chapters, we could suppose that because the married are more likely than the unmarried to be White and economically advantaged, they would be less likely to rely on relatives. After all, they need less help from family and friends, and the norms of reciprocity ensure they give less in return. The married are also more likely to be older, and perhaps older people are less interested in getting out. Similarly, marriage might isolate because the married are more likely to have children who may cause parents to cut back on other relationships. Structural explanations suggest that once we consider these characteristics—education, income, employment status, race/ethnicity, age, parental status—differences in the social ties by marital status will attenuate.

Analyses of the data, however, do not support these suppositions. In fact, differences in contact and assistance with relatives, friends, and neighbors emerge even if the married, never married, and previously married are the same age and race/ethnicity and have the same education, employment status, and income.

Similarly, our research shows that isolationist effects of marriage on extended family ties exist both among the childless and among parents of young children. Moreover, children partly reintegrate the married into networks of friends and neighbors. Married parents provide as much emotional and practical help to friends as single parents or childless singles; it is the married without children who give less. As Karen Hansen argues in *Not-So-Nuclear Families* (2005), dual earner parents, searching for ways to make childrearing feasible, turn to friends, neighbors, and extended family. And in the case of friends and neighbors, getting help typically means giving it in return. But help is only one way that people interact: Parents—single and married alike—"hang out" less with neighbors and friends than those without kids (married or not). Combining these effects, we still see a "marriage penalty" on relationships with friends and neighbors; it's just larger for the childless than for those with young children. Thus, in contrast to racial/ethnic differences that were primarily explained by structural factors, the isolationist effects of marriage persist even if we take structural factors—like the constraints and opportunities associated with economic circumstances or parenting—into account.

Culture

Emphasizing expectations and meanings, cultural explanations suggest that the isolating effects of marriage on social ties reach beyond its structural correlates, but are far from universal—it is primarily a contemporary phenomenon. Expectations and meanings vary across time and place. Anthropological studies of so-called "primitive societies"—hardly touched by industrialization or globalization—find that marriage is often used to expand rather than limit community ties. Extended kinship in such societies is the main source of support, and marriages are primarily forged between groups rather than between the two individuals. Rules prohibiting incest and promoting "marrying out" extend to distant relatives, ensuring that the families of married couples will rely economically and politically on a broad array of relatives. In such traditional societies, weddings are community events—they celebrate the newly formed alliances between extended families rather than the special relationship of the marital pair. Such societies don't have honeymoons—it is not appropriate to leave the community behind to go off on some private adventure. Marriage ensures communal integration in such societies.

Modern marriage is different. As the famous anthropologist Margaret Mead (1978, quoted in Andrews 1993: 315) put it: "Nobody has ever before asked the nuclear family to live all by itself in a box the way we do. With no relatives, no support, we've put it in an impossible situation." Contemporary marriage is based on cultural expectations of romantic love (Goode 1959)—which emphasizes the partners' focus on one another rather than on practical concerns of community survival. Spouses are expected to be "soulmates"—confidants and the main source of support for each other. As a recent Gallup poll finds, 94 percent of singles say their primary goal for marriage is finding a "soulmate" (Whitehead and Popenoe 2001). Consistent with that, contemporary weddings place more emphasis on individuals than community. As Andrew Cherlin argues (2009), weddings today celebrate romance and promote self-development, individual display, and personal achievement—decidedly private experiences—rather than the approval and alliances of extended families. And although the wedding may still have elements of a community ritual, the honeymoon is a decidedly private one. Honeymoons first developed in the nineteenth century when the idea of marriage as a private intimate relationship, set off from community life, began to take hold. Today, honeymoons of some kind are a nearly universal experience in the United States. As they go off on their honeymoon adventure, the starry-eyed couple is supposed to leave all other loved ones behind—the first step towards communal withdrawal.

Upon returning, they expect to reduce their reliance on relatives who may have supported them prior to marriage. Americans believe that couples should be able to make it on their own—both practically and emotionally. This does not mean that relatives or friends refuse to help the married when asked. It means that couples think that when they get married, they should be able to support and care for themselves. Many even postpone getting married until they think they can "make it on their own," even if that means not getting married at all. Since spouses are expected to be confidants for each other, the married are less likely than singles to call a sibling, parent, or friend to recount their day at work or their problems with kids. The married are also less able to spontaneously get together with friends without worrying that their spouse will feel emotionally deprived. And friends and family may feel less inclined to just "drop by" due to the risk of "interrupting something."

To be sure, cultural expectations of romantic love may also reduce social connections of the unmarried. Singles are likely to put much time and effort into finding a potential marital partner, which can dampen other social ties. In addition, single individuals may be hesitant to become too "dependent" on someone other than a potential "soulmate." For example, in Margaret Nelson's study of White rural single mothers (2005), she finds that they reserve some rights and privileges for a father regardless of whether they have specific men in mind. Consequently, these mothers experience mixed feelings about allowing grandmothers—whose help they may very much need—to assume the rights they think appropriate for a man, even if only an imagined or hoped for man.

As we saw in the previous chapter, material circumstances can push people to rely on extended family. In many ways, that might mean that the poor, minorities, and unmarried individuals are especially likely to feel forced to "do family" in ways that contradict their cultural beliefs and oftentimes feel ambivalent about it. Such ambivalence is generated when someone—whether married or not—must deviate from the script suggesting nuclear families should be self-sufficient and not rely on others for help. Thus, the cultural idea of a nuclear family dampens extended family ties as well as community ties for both the married and the unmarried. And it introduces ambivalence toward extended family ties.

Another Explanation: Self-Selection Processes

Some might argue that the reduction in social ties results more from self-selection into marriage rather than processes within marriage. For example, perhaps those lacking strong informal ties are especially likely to marry: For them, marriage might substitute for other relationships. Perhaps those deeply immersed in relationships with relatives and friends are less likely to get married because, to prevent the weakening of their relationships, those close to them may discourage them from getting married. But even if relatives and friends favor and promote marriage, intense ties to relatives may reduce the opportunity to meet a marital partner: Hanging out with close relatives all the time reduces one's chances of meeting a mate. Caregiving to relatives and friends also sometimes comes at the expense of care for partners and perhaps interferes with nuclear family stability.

Nevertheless, it is unlikely that differences between the married and unmarried can be fully attributed to self-selection. White (2001) presents some telling evidence in that regard: She finds that getting married leads to less contact and care among siblings whereas divorce produces more. Thus, it is likely that the differences between the married and the unmarried result *both* from self-selection into marriage as well as the dynamics that occur within marriage.

Conclusion

To be sure, most Americans—married or not—still live near their extended families. They want relationships with their elderly parents, siblings, aunts, uncles and cousins, see them occasionally, and feel guilty when they cannot help them. They bemoan their inability to maintain stronger ties. Yet today these ties are voluntary and sometimes get lost amidst the more pressing demands of marriage. Few anticipate that when they marry, they will not only choose but also likely circumscribe their social worlds.

Political and religious movements often recognize that marriage can undermine other relationships. Communal societies, like Oneida in the 19th century, rejected marriage because they viewed the "marriage spirit" as inimical to community life.

If any couple exhibited the marriage spirit, the community worked to break it up. More recently, Israeli kibbutzim have emphasized that the strength of the collectivity depended on a weakened marital and family life. Social movements also oftentimes depend on unmarried participants—social movement scholars call that "biographical availability." As Wiltfang and McAdam (1991) wrote, those who are married are less involved in social protest because marriage "implies a set of commitments that may supersede loyalties to the movement" (997). The Huk rebels in the Philippines imposed limits on marriage to assure that their members remain committed to the cause (Goodwin 1997). Or take the Catholic Church's stance on monks' and nuns' celibacy:

> [The Church] … stressed that ministers should abstain from marriage because the multiplicity of distractions originating in family life rendered it desirable for those in the service of the Church to be relieved from family care and anxiety.
>
> (Coser 1967: 200)

Many may believe, then, that the greater social involvement of singles is unsurprising. After all, marriages require a significant investment of time and energy that detracts from investments in other relationships. This may be especially true for dual-earner couples already strapped for time by the demands of two jobs. Moreover, some welcome this focus on the nuclear family; they suggest that involvement with relatives and friends is a poor substitute for involvement with a partner and children; that singles just get caught up in a restless chase for companionship that can be an exhausting affair. Some might assert that this difference between married and unmarried people means that for every additional hour a married woman spends with a loving husband, an unmarried woman might spend more hours in a fraught relationship with her brother or sister. Some might even insist that one of the benefits of marriages is that they provide individuals with an escape from wider ties and obligations.

To be sure, just as we should not romanticize marriages, we should not romanticize extended family and community ties. While isolationist tendencies of marriage can have negative consequences, there may also be some positive consequences. For example, marriage may lead to withdrawal from dangerous social groups such as gangs and criminal networks—what Putnam (2000) terms "a dark side of **social capital**." Sampson, Laub, and Wimer (2006), studying White men, found marriage reduces criminal activities and incarceration. Marriage may also lead to withdrawal from financially draining networks: By not having to help relatives or friends financially, married individuals might boost their own assets. Still, most of us agree that community ties are by and large a good thing. Thus, by ignoring the effects of marriage on extended family and community ties, we miss important *social* consequences that go far beyond individuals, couples, and their children.

For example, as the population ages, marriage may deprive elderly parents—who, ironically, often press their children to marry—of the help and support that they need. Marriage can also generate excessive burdens on those who are single, as they are expected to provide the care that their married siblings do not. In addition, as marriage becomes the only place where individuals look for support and comfort, marriage itself may become even more fragile. And children of such marriages might be disadvantaged as well; as Nobel prize-winning writer Pearl S. Buck put it:

> The lack of emotional security of our American young people is due, I believe, to their isolation from the larger family unit. No two people—no mere father and mother—as I have often said, are enough to provide emotional security for a child.
> (Buck 1967)

In addition, as movements to allow gay and lesbian marriages keep celebrating additional victories, gays and lesbians, once noted for their vibrant culture and community life, may also find themselves behind picket fences with fewer friends dropping by.

The isolating effects of marriage are felt across race and class. But because those with fewer economic resources are more likely to rely on extended family, these effects of marriage are particularly costly to them. Thus, not only is the focus on marriage a narrow vision but it may actually detract from the very resources—rooted outside the nuclear family and marriage—on which many Americans depend.

DISCUSSION QUESTIONS

1. What arguments do scholars make about the advantages and disadvantages of marriage? How can self-selection account for either the positive or negative effects of marriage?
2. What are the effects of marriage on extended families and broader community? What are the explanations for the effects of marriage on extended family ties? Which of these explanations do you find most convincing?
3. Compare your single friends or relatives to those who are married: Do you see more involvement with relatives, friends, or broader community among the single ones or the married ones? In your opinion, why do these differences appear?

VI: Social Policies and Families

ᵔᵕᵔᵕᵔ

As we come to the end of this book, it is time to assess how well we as a nation support our families. In Chapter IV, we listened to stories of nursing assistants who get a lot of help from relatives and often want to help them in return. Do our social policies make it easier for them to balance their numerous responsibilities? How does government policy define families? What kinds of assistance does it provide to families on the basis of this view? Do social policies and programs favor a nuclear family arrangement and what are the consequences of doing so?

Politicians often promise great support for families. Nevertheless, much U.S. policy that bears on families—whether inadequate provisions for affordable childcare, hospital regulations that now send home patients "quicker and sicker," or limited provisions for vacation or holidays—do not serve families very well. Many other countries, especially throughout Europe, offer much better childcare, medical care, and time off for vacations and holidays (Clawson and Gerstel 2002; Gornick and Meyers 2003). Moreover, U.S. family policy today often gives priority to marriage and the nuclear family while making the extended family all but invisible. This invisibility makes public policy even less effective than it would be otherwise. Policy based on the nuclear family works to the benefit of those already privileged.

There are numerous public policies that promote some aspects of marriage and the nuclear family while undermining extended families. This concluding chapter examines five such policies, including: (1) family and medical leaves; (2) Medicaid; (3) welfare reform; (4) policies on grandparents; (5) gay and lesbian marriage.

Family and Medical Leaves

In response to the entrance of growing numbers of women into the labor force, many in the United States fought for and won the passage of the Family and Medical Leave Act (FMLA) of 1993—the key U.S. policy in the area of family leave. Moving beyond prior legislation that allowed maternity leave, the FMLA mandates job leaves not only for workers' own serious personal illness, including maternity "disability," but also allow leaves to provide care for newborns or newly adopted children as well as for seriously ill children, spouses, or parents. The FMLA guarantees a 12-week job-protected leave with continuation of group health benefits and ensures restoration to the same job or an equivalent position following the leave.

Such leaves, however, are available only to public employees and those who work for private employers with 50 or more employees within a 75-mile radius. Therefore, most employers (95 percent) and many workers (45 percent) are *not* covered by the law. Further, leaves are only available to those who have worked for their employer for at least a year—making them inaccessible for the growing number of temporary workers. Finally, these federally mandated leaves are unpaid, and many simply can't afford to take them.

Though recognizing the compromises made along the way in getting the Act passed, most advocates hailed its passage, emphasizing both its **universalism** (especially its gender neutrality) and family friendliness as triumphs of progressive policy making. There is good reason, however, to be skeptical. Although gender neutrality in family leave taking was a primary goal of the FMLA, actual leave taking since the passage of the Act is far from gender neutral: It is overwhelmingly women (especially married) who say they need leaves, take leaves, and take longer leaves. And the leaves they take are more likely than men's to be for other people. These gender inequalities interact with race: It is White men who are particularly unlikely to take a family leave (Armenia and Gerstel 2006). Class position also affects the ability to take family leaves and the length of those leaves: While less affluent women are more likely to perceive a need for a family leave (Gerstel and McGonagle 1999), they take less time off than more affluent women (Albiston 2007). Low-wage workers also are significantly more likely to experience employer pressure to return to work when they do manage to take leaves. A number of FMLA characteristics explain these multiple inequities; these include assumptions about the family (that it includes two spouses, one of whom makes a "family wage") and assumptions about jobs (that they are full-time, long-term, and well-paid) which limit the range of those who can take advantage of it.

In the research on medical caregivers that we discussed in Chapter IV, Clawson and Gerstel found that, although the employers they studied were large enough to be covered by the FMLA, many nursing assistants were afraid to even ask for leave, even if their children were quite sick or their parents needed intensive personal care (Gerstel 2011). Sadly, they were caregivers who could not get time to care for those closest to them. As one nursing aide said:

> My mom had a heart attack, and she was in the hospital and I had to do the sixteen hours [at my job], nonstop, just like worried and what's goin' on, and I can't call out, 'cause I get fired.

Unfortunately, this is not an unusual case. Over 15 years after the passage of the Act, a national survey shows that between 23 percent and 46 percent of corporations that are legally required to follow the FMLA do not comply with it (Armenia, Gerstel, and Wing 2011). Moreover, the family that the Act is friendly to is a very particular kind. The original version of the bill only provided leave to heterosexual parents to care for young children. Eventual supporters of the bill, including AARP (formerly the American

Association of Retired Persons) and the U.S. Conference of Catholic Bishops, insisted the definition be broadened because they "liked the more inclusive notion of extended family and the concept of a multigenerational circle of care" (cited in Elving 1995: 78). As a result, elderly parents are now covered by the law. And in 2010, the Obama administration announced that the government will reinterpret the law in a way that will allow same-sex partners to take job leaves to give care to their partners' children. Limiting the Act's protections to parents, spouses or partners, and minor children still conforms to a narrow and biased view of the family. Everyone needs leaves from jobs to take care of those who are close to them. This is especially important for those less affluent because they often live with and help a wide range of kin, including grandparents, siblings, aunts, uncles, and cousins. And their relatives are unlikely to have the resources to purchase care. None of these family members are covered by the FMLA. Even fewer are covered by the push for paid leaves—which tend to be confined to nuclear families, that is, spouses and parents attending to minor children.

To be sure, the FMLA policy—for which so many fought so hard—*is* a major move forward. We should, however, assess the FMLA through a prism of other possibilities. Most European countries provide extensive paid family leave, usually universal, with job protection and substantial income replacement. Informed by these possibilities, U.S. activists continue to struggle to implement policy that covers a broader range of caregivers. Many of these struggles center on obtaining paid family leaves that would help alleviate the gender, racial, and class inequalities now built into the law.

Medicaid

Medicaid is another example of a policy that bears on families. It is a joint state and federal program that provides health insurance for low-income families with children and people with disabilities as well as long-term care for low-income elderly and disabled Americans. Because each state administers its own Medicaid plan, it varies from state to state.

As we have seen, care to ill, injured, or disabled individuals is often provided by extended kin. Family members who care for low-income relatives—whether for elderly mothers and fathers or disabled sisters or cousins—often say they feel caregiving "should stay in the family." In most states, however, Medicaid regulations only allow payment to caregivers who are non-family members. Here, unlike elsewhere, the definition of family expands: The Medicaid regulations include a long list of family members who *cannot* be paid to care for ill, injured, or disabled individuals. In practice, then, Medicaid discriminates against those who rely on extended families (Mutchler and Angel 2000). Some states do allow relatives to receive payment for giving care, but such family caregivers are paid very low hourly wages for this work, and they also feel stigmatized for accepting money to provide care to their family members (Stacey

2009). As Zelizer (2005) has argued, money and love are viewed as incompatible, even though those with little money need to rely on their families—especially extended families—as a strategy for survival.

"Welfare" Policy

In 1996, Congress passed and Clinton signed the Personal Responsibility and Work Opportunity Reconciliation Act (PRWORA)—"ending welfare as we know it."[1] The bill eliminated the federal entitlement program, Aid to Families with Dependent Children (AFDC), and created a new program called Temporary Assistance for Needy Families (TANF), which limits "welfare" to five years over a lifetime. The law explicitly establishes a particular ideology of family and work. Asserting that "marriage is the foundation of a successful society," the Act's official, stated purposes are not only to provide assistance to needy families with children but to: 1) end dependence by promoting employment *and* marriage; 2) gradually decrease out of wedlock birth; and 3) promote the formation of two parent families (PRWORA, Title I, sections 101, 401). As an alternative to welfare, the Act champions as equivalents paid work *or* marriage to an employed husband (preferring both).

Like the FMLA, TANF is written in gender-neutral language. But gender inequality in families and paid work shapes its actual impact: Not only are women much more likely to assume the primary responsibility for all sorts of caregiving, but on average, they also earn less than men. As a result, the reform champions the dependence of wives on husbands or at least fathers with paying jobs. But there are numerous flaws in this reasoning. First, where do these women find men to marry and support them? Furstenberg (2004) suggests that initiatives to persuade low-income women and men to marry misunderstand the nature of "resistance" to marriage. Most women with low income are not against marriage; they do not marry because they believe (and social science evidence supports them) that stable marriages depend on stable employment with decent wages. Many poor women delay marriage until they can find a trustworthy breadwinning mate (Edin and Kefalas 2005). In addition, many of those women who are subject to welfare mandates to marry and depend on biological fathers experience domestic and sexual abuse (Burton 2011). And since the mid-1970s, there has been a dramatic decline in real wages and labor force participation among young men with little education. Current initiatives provide few educational

---

1 We are using the term "welfare" to refer primarily to AFDC, The Personal Responsibility Act and TANF because this is the popular usage. But, we do so with some trepidation: Using the term welfare to describe only the receipt of state support by the poor may further marginalize the poor and make invisible all the advantages that the non-poor receive from the state (hence the recent development of the counter term, "corporate welfare").

and economic opportunities—instead, they promote marriages that are likely to end in divorce because of the economic stresses poor welfare recipients confront. Not only is there much reason to believe that the welfare reform cannot meet its official goal of supporting marriage, but such a goal is itself suspect.

Moreover, the state now compels "welfare" mothers to cooperate in identifying, tracking down, and collecting money from their children's biological fathers. In doing so, it insists on the economic dependence of mothers on the biological fathers of their children, rather than on the state. States are still struggling to set up procedures that comply with these new regulations. Many of the fathers cannot be located. Others simply do not have enough money to pay; overwhelmed by high child support orders, these fathers may avoid formal market earnings and thus pay nothing (Miller and Mincy 2009). As Mincy, Klempin, and Schmidt write:

> Recent reports suggest that child support default rates are rising during the Great Recession. … It seems merciless to insist on full compliance with child support during the longest recession in the postwar period, especially while forgiving debts accumulated on Wall Street and Main Street.
>
> (2011: 253)

In addition, some mothers give misleading information to the state's Child Support Enforcement in order to protect the identity of their children's fathers. Mothers mislead the welfare system, according to recent research, because state agencies rarely help them get the support they need to survive. These mothers also conceal information because the reporting of fathers, which may place them in jail, sometimes makes it impossible for these often poor men to continue to offer the financial support and in-kind assistance that they do in fact provide, if only sporadically (Hays 2004). Many of these disadvantaged men provide support to other relatives, especially their mothers, who receive inadequate support from governmental programs and might be helping out with the grandchildren (Mincy, Klempin, and Schmidt 2011). In fact, when they are in prison, about a fifth of incarcerated men rely on their parents and other relatives to care for their minor children (Raphael 2011). Thus, these disadvantaged men and their relatives depend on and care for extended family, though they are pressured to prioritize the nuclear family.

The effects of TANF are difficult to disentangle from other changes in the economy and tax policy. Its advocates point to its successes, especially the reduced caseload and dramatic increases in employment among those previously on welfare (Nightingale 2002; Pear 2004). Many of the jobs that former "welfare mothers" find, however, are unstable, providing low wages with minimal chance for mobility (Jencks and Swingle 2000). Consequently, most who find jobs do not leave poverty (Blalock, Tiller, and Monroe 2004). Instead, they are forced to shoulder the increased hardships of combining employment with unpaid carework. Thus, the employment requirements of welfare reform simultaneously restrict and devalue the care provided by poor mothers, intensifying the already substantial obstacles they face in raising their children (Weigt 2006).

While claiming to strengthen the family, welfare reform makes it especially hard for poor mothers to give care to their loved ones—be they young or old. More than a quarter of welfare recipients work mostly at night and over half struggle to coordinate work schedules with childcare. Moreover, TANF legislation further exaggerates these problems by reducing extended families' ability to provide support to each other (Oliker 2000). Even though under AFDC, welfare benefits were provided to individuals, this money oftentimes benefitted broader families and communities as well. Thus, when the assistance is cut for an individual single mother, the loss of that money serves as a loss not only to her and her children, but to her entire network of relatives and supportive friends. As a result, welfare leavers lose not only money, time, and services but also informal support, especially since they are less able to give care and "giving is as constitutive of communal networks [among the poor] as getting" (Oliker 2000: 178). And the low wage job market they enter leaves most women financially incapable of replacing the care they once provided with purchased services. In seeking to strengthen nuclear families, then, this reform reduces the quality of care that children of welfare recipients get, forces women into abusive marriages and marriages that are likely to end in divorce, and weakens extended family ties.

Moreover, it also intensifies inequality between families by reinforcing the ability of some families to exercise power over other families. A significant number of jobs these poor women find are service jobs to provide care in and out of households—including childcare, cleaning services, or care in nursing homes (Macdonald 2011). These jobs typically provide low wages, often below the poverty line. The welfare reform, then, helps maintain the position of those affluent families that can obtain cheap services from those forced off welfare.

Overall, welfare policy is linked to a broad spectrum of family and work issues. We need, therefore, to consider a multitude of alternative policies to alleviate the problems of the poor single mothers who rely on it. Rather than focus on encouraging these mothers to pull themselves up by their bootstraps, these policies should have two primary targets for change: The employment structure and the taken for granted, undervalued, and unpaid nature of carework. Moreover, instead of trying to force marriage upon welfare mothers, these policies should recognize the importance of extended family members in their lives and support rather than discourage these broader networks.

Policies on Grandparents

Policies on grandparents offer another important example of the limits of U.S. family policy. An increasing number of children reside with their grandparents: Pew Research

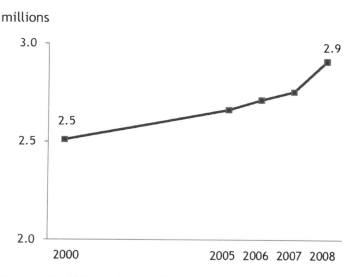

millions

Figure 6.1 Sharp increase in children with grandparent caregivers since 2007.
Note: Includes children who live with a grandparent responsible for most of their daily needs.
Source: Pew Research Center (2010c) report, "Since the Start of the Great Recession, More Children Raised by Grandparents."
Available from: http://pewsocialtrends.org/files/2010/10/764-children-raised-by-grandparents.pdf.
Based on Pew Research Center calculations of Decennial Census and American Community Survey data.

Center (2010c) reports that one child in ten lives with a grandparent, and this share not only has steadily increased over the past decade but also increased sharply during the "Great Recession" (see Figure 6.1). About forty percent of children who live with grandparents are being raised *primarily* by these grandparents, and this number has also increased dramatically during the Great Recession.

Yet, few scholars or policy makers discuss the need for the **institutionalization** of children's relationships with grandparents, reflecting a bias in favor of nuclear family ties. In the United States, grandparents have no legal responsibility or authority to care for their grandchildren unless they are granted that authority by a court (Letiecq, Bailey, and Porterfield 2008), which requires that individuals approach the court—an often costly, time consuming, and frightening experience. This lack of institutionalization can be a problem for the growing number of grandparents who become primary caregivers to their grandchildren. Though taking informal responsibility for their grandchildren, these grandparents typically have no legal authority.

In contrast, there are examples of progressive policies with regard to grandparenting in a number of European countries. Such policies recognize the roles grandparents play in many families and facilitate their involvement—for example, by allowing grandparents to take leaves to take care of grandchildren or by allowing parental leaves or allowances to be transferred to grandparents.

Gay and Lesbian Marriage

The gay–lesbian movement is now pouring resources into the promotion of same-sex marriages instead of other issues. Recently, economist Lee Badgett, in her book, *When Gay People Get Married* (2009), asked the interesting question: Does the implementation of same-sex marriage change gays or does it change marriage? Talking to a public policy audience and hoping to obtain popular support for same-sex marriage, Badgett argues that marriage changes gays, but gays do not change marriage. If she is right, then the push for same-sex marriage that has absorbed so many of the resources of the LGBTQ (lesbian, gay, bisexual, transgender, and queer) movement may serve to further undermine a once vibrant community. As Duggan (2003) argues, this push entails a narrow vision of marriage which administers "a kind of political sedative ... we get marriage and the military and then we go home and cook dinner, forever" (62).

Other gay and lesbian activists have also questioned the role of marriage on LGBTQ agenda by emphasizing that marriage disproportionately privileges some relationships over others—including those with relatives. As Ettelbrick wrote:

> Marriage creates a two-tier system that allows the state to regulate relationships. It has become a facile mechanism for employers to dole out benefits, for businesses to provide special deals and incentives, and for the law to make distinctions in distributing meager public funds. None of these entities bothers to consider the relationship among people; the love, respect and need to protect that exists among all kinds of family members. Rather, a simple certificate of the state, regardless of whether the spouses love, respect, or even see each other on a regular basis, dominates and is supported. None of this dynamic will change if gay men and lesbians are given the option to marry.
>
> (Ettelbrick 1998: 484)

Scholars like Ettelbrick suggest that rather than advocating for gays and lesbians to have a right to marry in order to access benefits that are tied to marriage, we should be advocating for decoupling those benefits from marriage to ensure that people have access to those benefits regardless of their marital status. A committed and caring relationship between two romantic partners should not be valued more than a committed and caring relationship between an aging parent and an adult child, or between two siblings.

Conclusion

Throughout this book, we have seen that many Americans rely on extended family members for all kinds of support and help. Moreover, we have seen that such reliance is not spread equitably across the population: Women, people of color, and those with fewer material resources are more likely to give and get this care.

Extended family care is important; indeed, it is the way many people in our society manage to survive. But as this chapter shows, we as a nation are unsupportive of extended families. When we support families, our policies support marriage and nuclear families rather than extended families. The evidence presented in this book clearly demonstrates that such policies discriminate against women, racial/ethnic minorities, and the poor.

In addition to the particular policies described above, there are numerous other examples: For instance, substance abuse rehabilitation programs often provide arrangements for childcare while a parent participates in the program, but they do not provide arrangements for care given to extended kin, such as elderly parents (Black and Hardesty 2000). Similarly, inheritance and housing laws, social security and hospital visitation policies, as well as prison programs designed to maintain and rehabilitate families all have provisions for nuclear family members but neglect concerns of extended families.

Of course, we must take care of our young children and our partners. And many Americans agree that gays and lesbians should have the same rights and opportunities as everyone else. But that's not enough. By focusing on the nuclear family and ignoring its various extensions, we limit our understanding of how family life in the United States operates, particularly among those with few economic resources. As a result, we weaken our explanatory models and are in danger of making bad policy. Social policies that focus on nuclear families and overlook extended family obligations may introduce, reproduce, or even increase gender, racial/ethnic, and class inequalities. To create unbiased, inclusive policy, we must attend to the realities and practices of families and the care they actually give and get rather than confine our policies to narrow biological or marriage-based conceptions of who should count as family.

DISCUSSION QUESTIONS

1. In what ways do U.S. social policies make family a privilege of an affluent minority rather than a right for most people, regardless of their race or class?
2. How does U.S. social policy reinforce gender inequalities?
3. Many people today support gay and lesbian marriage while some argue there may be some negative consequences of legalizing these marriages. Present both arguments.

References

Albiston, Catherine. 2007. "Institutional Perspectives on Law, Work, and Family." *Annual Review of Law and Social Science* 3: 397–426.

Alvirez, David, and Frank D. Bean. 2006. "The Mexican American Family." Pp. 272–292 in *Ethnic Families in America: Patterns of Variance*, eds. Charles Mindel and Robert Habenstein. New York: Elsevier North-Holland Inc.

Anderson, Elijah. 1990. *Streetwise: Race, Class, and Change in an Urban Community*. Chicago, IL: University of Chicago Press.

Andrews, Robert. 1993. *The Columbia Dictionary of Quotations*. New York: Columbia University Press.

Armenia, Amy, and Naomi Gerstel. 2006. "Family Leaves, the FMLA, and Gender Neutrality: The Intersection of Race and Gender." *Social Science Research* 35: 871–891.

Armenia, Amy, Naomi Gerstel, and Coady Wing. 2010. *Estimating and Predicting Compliance with the FMLA: Pressures from Above and Below*. Accessed online at http://economix.blogs.nytimes.com/2010/01/25/family-leaves-right-or-privilege

Aschenbrenner, Joyce. 1975. *Lifelines: Black Families in Chicago*. New York: Holt, Rinehart and Winston.

Baca Zinn, Maxine, and Barbara Wells. 2000. "Diversity within Latino Families: New Lessons for Family Social Science." Pp. 252–273 in *Handbook of Family Diversity*, eds. D. H. Demo, K. R. Allen, and M. A. Fine. New York: Oxford University Press.

Badgett, M. V. Lee. 2009. *When Gay People Get Married*. New York: New York University Press.

Barrett, Michelle, and Mary McIntosh. 1982. *The Anti-Social Family*. London: Verso Press.

Belkin, Lisa. 2003. "The Opt-Out Revolution." *New York Times Sunday Magazine* (October 26): 42–47, 58, 85–86.

Bengston, Vern L. 2001. "Beyond the Nuclear Family: The Increasing Importance of Multigenerational Bonds." *Journal of Marriage and Family* 63: 1–16.

Black, Timothy, and Monica Hardesty. 2000. "The Trajectory of Recovery among Drug Dependent Puerto Rican Mothers." *Advances in Medical Sociology* 7: 193–213.

Blalock, Lydia L., Vicky R. Tiller, and Pamela Monroe. 2004. "'They Get You Out of Courage': Persistent Deep Poverty among Former Welfare-Reliant Women." *Family Relations* 53: 127–137.

Bourdieu, Pierre. 1986. "The Forms of Capital." Pp. 241–258 in *Handbook of Theory and Research for the Sociology of Education*, ed. John G Richardson. New York: Greenwood Press.

Boushey, Heather. 2005. *Are Women Opting Out? Debunking the Myth.* Briefing Paper, Center for Economic and Policy Research. Accessed online at www.cepr.net/documents/publications/opt_out_2005_11_2.pdf

Brines, Julie. 1994. "Economic Dependency, Gender and the Division of Labor at Home." *American Journal of Sociology* 100: 652–688.

Buck, Pearl Sydenstricker. 1967. *To My Daughters, with Love.* New York: John Day Co.

Burton, Linda. 2011. "Journeys to the Altar: The Intimate Union Pattern of Low Income Urban and Rural Mothers." Paper presented at the Center for Research on Families, University of Massachusetts. Amherst, MA.

Campbell, Lori D., Ingrid Arnet Connidis, and Lorraine Davies. 1999. "Sibling Ties in Later Life: A Social Network Analysis." *Journal of Family Issues* 20: 113–148.

Carrington, Christopher. 1999. *No Place Like Home: Relationships and Family Life among Lesbians and Gay Men.* Chicago, IL: University of Chicago Press.

Cherlin, Andrew. 2009. *The Marriage-Go-Round: The State of Marriage and the Family in America Today.* New York: Knopf.

Chodorow, Nancy. 1978. *The Reproduction of Mothering: Psychoanalysis and the Sociology of Gender.* Berkeley: University of California Press.

Christakis, Nicholas A., and James H. Fowler. 2009. *Connected: The Surprising Power of Our Social Networks and How They Shape Our Lives.* New York: Little, Brown and Company.

Clawson, Dan, and Naomi Gerstel. 2002. "Caring for Our Young: Child Care in Europe and the United States." *Contexts* 1 (4): 28–35.

Clawson, Dan, Naomi Gerstel, and Jill Crocker. 2009. "Employers Meet Families: Gender, Class, and Paid Work Hour Differences among U.S. Medical Workers." *Social Indicators Research* 93: 185–189.

Clemetson, Lynette. 2006. "Work vs. Family, Complicated by Race." *New York Times* (February 9): G1.

Cohen, Patricia. 2010. "'Culture of Poverty' Makes a Comeback." *New York Times* (October 18): A1.

Cohen, Philip. 2011. *Multigenerational Families, Recession Studies.* Accessed online at http://family-inequality.wordpress.com/2011/01/03/multigenerational-families-recession-studies/

Collins, Patricia Hill. 2000. *Black Feminist Thought: Knowledge, Consciousness, and the Politics of Empowerment (2nd ed.).* New York: Routledge.

Coser, Lewis. 1967. "Greedy Organizations." *European Journal of Sociology* 8: 196-215.

Coser, Lewis, and Rose Coser. 1974. *Greedy Institutions: Patterns of Undivided Commitment.* New York: Free Press.

Damaske, Sarah. 2011. "A 'Major Career Woman': How Women Develop Early Expectations about Work." *Gender and Society* 25: 409–430.

Duggan, Lisa. 2003. *The Twilight of Equality?: Neoliberalism, Cultural Politics and the Attack on Democracy.* New York: Beacon Press Books.

Durkheim, Émile. [1897] 1966. *Suicide: A Study in Sociology.* Translated by John A. Spaulding and George Simpson. New York: Free Press.

Edin, Kathryn, and Maria Kefalas. 2005. *Promises I Can Keep: Why Poor Women Put Motherhood Before Marriage.* Berkeley: University of California Press.

Edin, Kathryn, Laura Tach, and Ronald Mincy. 2009. "Claiming Fatherhood: Race and the Dynamics of Paternal Involvement among Unmarried Fathers." *The ANNALS of the American Academy of Political and Social Science* 621: 149–177.

Elving, Ronald. 1995. *Conflict and Compromise: How Congress Makes the Law*. New York: Touchstone.

Epstein, Cynthia Fuchs. 1988. *Deceptive Distinctions: Sex, Gender and the Social Order*. New Haven, CT: Yale University Press.

Ettelbrick, Paula. 1998. "Since When is Marriage a Path to Liberation?" Pp. 481–486 in *Families in the U.S.: Kinship and Domestic Politics*, eds. Karen V. Hansen and Anita Ilta Garey. Philadelphia, PA: Temple University Press.

Fernandez Mendez, Eugenio. 1993. *Art and Mythology of the Taino Indians of the Greater West Indies*. Carolina, PR: Esmaco Printers Corp.

Frazier, E. Franklin. 1932. *The Negro Family in Chicago*. Chicago, IL: University of Chicago Press.

Furstenberg, Frank F. 2004. "The Fading Dream: Prospects for Marriage in the Inner City." Pp. 224–246 in *Problem of the Century: Racial Stratification in the United States*, eds. Elijah Anderson and Douglas S. Massey. New York: Russell Sage Foundation.

Galinsky, Ellen, Families and Work Institute, Louis Harris and Associates, and the Whirlpool Foundation. 1995. *Women: The New Providers: A Study of Women's Views on Family, Work, Society and the Future*. Benton Harbor, MI: Whirlpool Foundation.

Gerson, Kathleen. 2010. *The Unfinished Revolution: How a New Generation is Reshaping Family, Work, and Gender in America*. New York: Oxford University Press.

Gerstel, Naomi. 2000. "The Third Shift: Gender and Care Work Outside the Home." *Qualitative Sociology* 23: 467–483.

———. 2011. "Rethinking Families and Community: The Color, Class, and Centrality of Extended Kin Ties." *Sociological Forum* 26: 1–20.

Gerstel, Naomi, Dan Clawson, and Dana Huyser. 2007. "Explaining Job Hours of Physicians, Nurses, EMTs, and Nursing Assistants: Gender, Class, Jobs, and Families." Pp. 369–401 in *Workplace Temporalities (Research in the Sociology of Work, volume 17)*, ed. Beth A. Rubin. Amsterdam: Elsevier/JAI Press.

Gerstel, Naomi, and Sally Gallagher. 1994. "Caring for Kith and Kin: Gender, Employment, and the Privatization of Care." *Social Problems* 41: 519–539.

Gerstel, Naomi, and Kate McGonagle. 1999. "Job Leaves and the Limits of the Family and Medical Leave Act: The Effects of Gender, Race and Family," *Work and Occupations* 26: 510–534.

Gerstel, Naomi, and Natalia Sarkisian. 2006. "Marriage: The Good, the Bad, and the Greedy." *Contexts* 5 (4): 16–21.

———. 2007. "Intergenerational Care and the Greediness of Adult Children's Marriages." Pp. 153–188 in *Interpersonal Relations across the Life Course: Advances in Life Course Research, volume 12*, eds. Timothy J. Owens and J. Jill Suitor. Greenwich, CT: Elsevier/JAI Press.

———. 2008. "The Color of Family Ties: Race, Class, Gender, and Extended Family Involvement." Pp. 447–453 in *American Families: A Multicultural Reader. 2nd edition*, eds. Stephanie Coontz, Maya Parson, and Gabrielle Raley. New York: Routledge.

Goode, William. 1959. "The Theoretical Importance of Love." *American Sociological Review* 24: 38–47.

Goodwin, Jeff. 1997. "The Libidinal Constitution of a High-Risk Social Movement: Affectual Ties and Solidarity in the Huk Rebellion, 1946 to 1954." *American Sociological Review* 62: 53–69.

Gornick, Janet C., and Marcia K. Meyers. 2003. *Families That Work: Policies for Reconciling Parenthood and Employment*. New York: Russell Sage Foundation.

Greenstein, Theodore N. 2000. "Economic Dependence, Gender and the Division of Labor in the Home: A Replication and Extension." *Journal of Marriage and Family* 62: 322–335.

Gubrium, Jaber F., and James A. Holstein. 1990. *What Is Family?* Mountain View, CA: Mayfield.

Gutman, Herbert G. 1976. *The Black Family in Slavery and Freedom, 1750–1925*. New York: Vintage.

Handel, Gerald, Spencer E. Cahill, and Frederick Elkin. 2007. *Children and Society*. New York: Oxford University Press.

Hansen, Karen. 2005. *Not-So-Nuclear Families: Class, Gender, and Networks of Care*. New Brunswick, NJ: Rutgers University Press.

Haskins, Ron. 2009. "Moynihan Was Right: Now What?" *The ANNALS of the American Academy of Political and Social Science* 621: 281–314.

Haxton, Clarisse, and Kristen Harknett. 2009. "Racial and Gender Differences in Kin Support: A Mixed Methods Study of African American and Hispanic Couples." *Journal of Family Issues* 30: 1019–1040.

Hays, Sharon. 1996. *The Cultural Contradictions of Motherhood*. New Haven, CT: Yale University Press.

———. 2004. *Flat Broke with Children: Women in the Age of Welfare Reform*. New York: Oxford University Press.

Heymann, Jody S. 2000. *The Widening Gap: Why America's Working Families Are in Jeopardy—and What Can Be Done About It*. New York: Basic Books.

Hochschild, Arlie Russell, with Anne Machung. 1997. *The Second Shift: Working Parents and the Revolution at Home*. New York: Avon Books.

Hochschild, Arlie Russell. 2009. "The State of Family, Class, and Culture." *New York Times* (October 18): BR27.

Jencks, Christopher, and Joseph Swingle. 2000. "Without a Net." *The American Prospect*, 11 (4): 37–41.

Kahn, Joan, Brittany McGill, and Suzanne Bianchi. 2011. "Help to Family and Friends: Are There Gender Differences at Older Ages?" *Journal of Marriage and Family* 73: 77–92.

Kaplan, Elaine Bell. 1997. *Not Our Kind of Girl: Unraveling the Myths of Black Teenage Motherhood*. Berkeley, CA: University of California Press.

Landry, Bart. 2002. *Black Working Wives: Pioneers of the American Family Revolution*. Berkeley: University of California Press.

Lareau, Annette. 2003. *Unequal Childhoods: Class, Race, and Family Life*. Berkeley: University of California Press.

Lempert, Lora Bex. 1999. "Other Fathers: An Alternative Perspective on Black Community Caring." Pp. 189–201 in *The Black Family: Essays and Studies*, edited by Robert Staples. Belmont, CA: Wadsworth.

Letiecq, Bethany, Sandra J. Bailey, and Fonda Porterfield. 2008. "'We Have No Rights, We Get No Help' The Legal and Policy Dilemmas Facing Grandparent Caregivers." *Journal of Family Issues* 29: 995–1012.

Lewis, Oscar. 1965. *La Vida: A Puerto Rican Family in the Culture of Poverty, San Juan and New York*. New York: Random House.

Macdonald, Cameron Lynne. 2011. *Shadow Mothers: Nannies, Au Pairs, and the Micropolitics of Mothering*. Berkeley: University of California Press.

McDonald, Katrina Bell, and Elizabeth M. Armstrong. 2001. "De-Romanticizing Black Intergenerational Support: The Questionable Expectations of Welfare Reform." *Journal of Marriage and the Family* 63: 213–223.

Menjivar, Cecilia. 1997. "Immigrant Kinship Networks and the Impact of the Receiving Context: Salvadorans in San Francisco in the Early 1990s." *Social Problems* 44: 104–123.

———. 2000. *Fragmented Ties: Salvadoran Immigrant Networks in America*. Berkeley: University of California Press.

Miller, Daniel P., and Ronald B. Mincy. 2009. *The Effects of Child Support Arrears on Formal and Informal Labor Force Participation*. New York: Center for Research on Fathers, Children, and Family Well-Being, School of Social Work, Columbia University.

Mincy, Ronald B., Serena Klempin, and Heather Schmidt. 2011. "Income Support Policies for Low-Income Men and Noncustodial Fathers: Tax and Transfer Programs." *The ANNALS of the American Academy of Political and Social Science* 635: 240–261.

Mirandé, Alfredo. 1997. *Hombres y Machos: Masculinity and Latino Culture*. Boulder, CO: Westview.

Moynihan, Daniel P. 1965. *The Negro Family: A Case for National Action*. Washington, DC: Government Printing Office.

Musick, Marc A., John Wilson, and William B. Bynum, Jr. 2000. "Race and Formal Volunteering: The Differential Effects of Class and Religion." *Social Forces* 78: 1539–1571.

Mutchler, Jan E., and Jacqueline L. Angel. 2000. "Policy Development and the Older Latino Population in the 21st Century." *Journal of Aging and Social Policy* 11 (2–3): 177–188.

Nelson, Margaret. 2005. *The Social Economy of Single Motherhood: Raising Children in Rural America*. New York: Routledge.

Newman, Katherine S. 1999. *No Shame in My Game: The Working Poor in the Inner City*. New York: Alfred A. Knopf, Inc. and Russell Sage Foundation.

Nightingale, Demetra Smith. 2002. "Work Opportunities for People Leaving Welfare." Pp. 103–120 in *Welfare Reform: The Next Act*, eds. Alan Weil and Kenneth Finegold. Washington, DC: Urban Institute Press.

Obama, Barack. 2008. *Father's Day Speech*. Accessed online at http://articles.cnn.com/2008-06-27/politics/obama.fathers.ay_1_foundation-black-children-rock

Oliker, Stacey J. 2000. "Examining Care at Welfare's End." Pp. 167–185 in *Care Work: Gender, Labor, and Welfare State*, ed. Madonna Harrington Meyer. London: Routledge.

Osborne, Cynthia, Wendy D. Manning, and Pamela J. Smock. 2007. "Married and Cohabiting Parents' Relationship Stability: A Focus on Race and Ethnicity." *Journal of Marriage and Family* 69: 1345–1366.

Parker-Pope, Tara. 2010. "Now, Dad Feels as Stressed as Mom." *The New York Times* (June 20): WK1.

Parsons, Talcott, and Robert Bales. 1955. *Family, Socialization and Interaction Process*. Glencoe, IL: Free Press.

Paschal, Angelia M. 2006. *Voices of African American Teen Fathers: "I'm Doing What I Got to Do."* New York: Haworth Press.

Patterson, Orlando. 1998. *Rituals of Blood: Consequences of Slavery in Two American Centuries.* Washington, DC: Civitas/Counterpoint.

Pear, Robert. 2004. "Despite the Sluggish Economy, Welfare Rolls Actually Fell." *New York Times* (March 22): A21.

Perry-Jenkins, Maureen. 2004. "The Time and Timing of Work: Unique Challenges Facing Low-Income Families." Pp. 107–116 in *Work-Family Challenges for Low-Income Parents and Their Children*, eds. Ann Crouter and Alan Booth. Mahwah, NJ: Lawrence Erlbaum Associates.

Personal Responsibility and Work Opportunity Reconciliation Act of 1996. Pub. L. no. 104–193, 110 Stat. 2105.

Pew Research Center. 2010a. *The Decline of Marriage and Rise of New Families.* November 18. Accessed online at http://pewsocialtrends.org/files/2010/11/pew-social-trends-2010-families.pdf

———. 2010b. *The Return of the Multi-Generational Family Household.* March 18. Accessed online at http://pewsocialtrends.org/2010/03/18/the-return-of-the-multi-generational-family-household/

———. 2010c. *Since the Start of the Great Recession, More Children Raised by Grandparents.* September 9. Accessed online at http://pewsocialtrends.org/files/2010/10/764-children-raised-by-grandparents.pdf

———. 2010d. *Pew Hispanic Center Country of Origin Profiles, 2008.* Accessed online at http://pewhispanic.org/data/origins

Popenoe, David. 1993. "American Family Decline, 1960-1990: A Review and Appraisal." *Journal of Marriage and the Family* 55: 527–542.

Powell, Brian, Catherine Bolzendahl, Claudia Geist, and Lala Carr Steelman. 2010. *Counted Out: Same-Sex Relations and Americans' Definitions of Family.* New York: Russell Sage Foundation.

Putnam, Robert D. 2000. *Bowling Alone: The Collapse and Revival of American Community.* New York: Simon & Schuster.

Raphael, Steven. 2011. "Incarceration and Prisoner Reentry in the United States." *The ANNALS of the American Academy of Political and Social Science* 635: 192–215.

Raspberry, William. 2005. "Why Our Black Families Are Failing." *The Washington Post* (July 25): A19.

Riley, Matilda White, and John W. Riley, Jr. 1993. "Connections: Kin and Cohort." Pp. 169–189 in *The Changing Contract Across Generations*, eds. Vern L. Bengtson and W. Andrew Achenbaum. New York: Aldine de Gruyter.

Rogler, Lloyd F., and Rosemary Santana Cooney. 1984. *Puerto Rican Families in New York City: Intergenerational Processes.* Maplewood, NJ: Waterfront Press.

Roschelle, Anne R. 1997. *No More Kin: Exploring Race, Class, and Gender in Family Networks.* Thousand Oaks, CA: Sage Publications.

Sampson, Robert J., John Laub, and Christopher Wimer. 2006. "Does Marriage Reduce Crime? A Counterfactual Approach to Within Individual Causal Effects?" *Criminology* 44: 465–508.

Sarkisian, Natalia. 2007. "Street Men, Family Men: Race and Men's Extended Family Involvement." *Social Forces* 86: 763–794.

Sarkisian, Natalia, and Naomi Gerstel. 2004a. "Explaining the Gender Gap in Help to Parents: The Importance of Employment." *Journal of Marriage and the Family* 66: 431–451.

———. 2004b. "Kin Support Among Blacks and Whites: Race and Family Organization." *American Sociological Review* 69: 812–837.

———. 2008. "Till Marriage Do Us Part: Adult Children's Relationships with Parents." *Journal of Marriage and Family* 70: 360–376.

Sarkisian, Natalia, Mariana Gerena, and Naomi Gerstel. 2006. "Extended Family Ties among Mexicans, Puerto Ricans, and Whites: Superintegration or Disintegration?" *Family Relations* 55: 331–344.

———. 2007. "Extended Family Integration among Euro and Mexican Americans: Ethnicity, Gender, and Class." *Journal of Marriage and Family* 69: 40–54.

Shows, Carla, and Naomi Gerstel. 2009. "Fathering, Class, and Gender: A Comparison of Physicians and EMTs." *Gender & Society* 23: 161–187.

Slater, Phillip. 1963. "On Social Regression." *American Sociological Review* 28: 339–364.

Small, Mario Luis, David J. Harding, and Michèle Lamont. 2010. "Reconsidering Culture and Poverty." *The ANNALS of the American Academy of Political and Social Science* 629: 6–27.

Stacey, Clare L. 2009. *Stigmatized Labors: The Meaning of Work for Paid Family Caregivers.* Paper presented at the Carework conference. San Francisco, CA.

Stacey, Judith. 1997. *In the Name of the Family: Rethinking Family Values in the Postmodern Age.* Boston: Beacon Press.

———. 2011. *Unhitched: Love, Marriage, and Family Values from West Hollywood to Western China.* New York: New York University Press.

Stack, Carol B. 1974. *All Our Kin: Strategies for Survival in a Black Community.* New York: Harper & Row.

Stoll, Michael A. 2001. "Race, Neighborhood Poverty, and Participation in Voluntary Associations." *Sociological Forum* 16: 529–557.

Stone, Pamela. 2007. *Opting Out: Why Women Really Quit Careers and Head Home.* Berkeley: University of California Press.

Sudarkasa, Niara. 1996. *The Strength of Our Mothers: African & African American Women and Families: Essays and Speeches.* Trenton, NJ: Africa World Press.

Swidler, Ann. 2001. *Talk of Love: How Culture Matters.* Chicago, IL: University of Chicago Press.

Taylor, Robert J., Linda M. Chatters, and James S. Jackson. 1997. "Changes Over Time in Support Network Involvement Among Black Americans." Pp. 293–316 in *Family Life in Black America*, eds. Robert Joseph Taylor, James S. Jackson, and Linda Marie Chatters. Thousand Oaks, CA: Sage Publications.

U.S. Census Bureau. 2011a. *Living Arrangements of Children: 2009.* Accessed online at http://www.census.gov/prod/2011pubs/p70-126.pdf

———. 2011b. *Income, Poverty, and Health Insurance Coverage in the United States: 2010.* Accessed online at http://www.census.gov/prod/2011pubs/p60-239.pdf

———. 2011c. *Statistical Abstract of the United States: 2012 (131st Edition).* Accessed online at http://www.census.gov/compendia/statab

———. 2010. *Census Bureau Reports Families with Children Increasingly Face Unemployment.* Washington, DC: U.S. Department of Commerce. Accessed online at http://www.census.gov/newsroom/releases/archives/families_households/cb10-08.html

Walker, Alexis. 2001. "Conceptual Perspectives on Gender and Family Caregiving." Pp. 34–48 in *Gender, Families and Elder Care*, eds. Jeffrey W. Dwyer and Raymond Coward. Thousand Oaks, CA: Sage.

Weigt, Jill. 2006. "Compromises to Carework: The Social Organization of Mothers' Experiences in the Low-Wage Labor Market after Welfare Reform." *Social Problems* 53: 332–351.

West, Candace, and Don H. Zimmerman. 1987. "Doing Gender." *Gender & Society* 1: 125–151.

White, Lynn K. 2001. "Sibling Relationships over the Life Course: A Panel Analysis." *Journal of Marriage and the Family* 63: 555–568.

White, Lynn K., and Agnes Riedmann. 1992. "Ties among Adult Siblings." *Social Forces* 71: 85–102.

Whitehead, Barbara Dafoe, and David Popenoe. 2001. "Who Wants To Marry a Soul Mate? New Survey Findings on Young Adults' Attitudes about Love and Marriage." Pp. 6–16 in *The State of Our Unions 2001: The Social Health of Marriage in America*. Piscataway, NJ: The National Marriage Project.

Wikipedia. 2011. *Family Values.* Accessed online at http://en.wikipedia.org/wiki/Family_values

Wiltfang, Gregory L., and Doug McAdam. 1991. "The Costs and Risks of Social Activism: A Study of Sanctuary Movement Activism." *Social Forces* 69: 987-1010.

Weston, Kath. 1991. *Families We Choose.* New York: Columbia University Press.

Zelizer, Viviana. 2005. *The Purchase of Intimacy.* Princeton, NJ: Princeton University Press.

Glossary/Index

A

Aid to Families with Dependent Children (AFDC) 49, 51
Albiston, Catherine 47
All Our Kin 20
Alvirez, David 19
American Sociological Review 3
Anderson, Elijah 21, 28
Andrews, Robert 42
Angel, Jacqueline 48
Anti-Social Family 37
Armenia, Amy 47
Armstrong, Elizabeth 21, 28
Aschenbrenner, Joyce 26

B

Baca Zinn, Maxine 15
Badgett, Lee 53
Bailey, Sandra 52
Bales, Robert 3
Barrett, Michelle 37
Bean, Frank 19
Belkin, Lisa 5
Bengtson, Vern 34–35
Bianchi, Suzanne 9
biology 7, 40
births to unmarried women 14, 16, 18
Black families
    births to unmarried women 16
    children living with a single parent 16–17
    cultural deficiency model and 25, 26
    cultural resiliency model and 26–27

"disorganization" argument and 12–14, 23
education, income and poverty rates 30–31
marital status 15–16
men in 14, 20, 21, 22, 23
structural destruction model and 27–28
structural resiliency model and 28
"superorganization" argument and 18–20
and support for extended kin 22–23, 31
women-centered 13, 14, 20–21, 25
work–life balance 19
Black, Timothy 54
Blalock, Lydia 50
Boushey, Heather 5
Brines, Julie 10
Buck, Pearl S. 45
Burton, Linda 49
Bynum, William 26

C
Campbell, Lori 6
Carework: The work of providing paid and unpaid care—from practical to emotional—that maintains children, the elderly, the sick, and the disabled in families, workplaces, and broader communities 3
difficulties in obtaining family leave for 47
gender differences in 6–10
of grandparents 51–52
welfare reform and impact on 50–51
Carrington, Christopher 9
Chatters, Linda 23
Cherlin, Andrew 42
children
adult children 2, 3, 6, 30, 32, 37–38
living in a single-parent household 16–17
raised by grandparents 34–35, 51–52
young children 2–3, 54
Chodorow, Nancy 7
Christakis, Nicholas 36
class
black middle-class 19
cultural deficiency model 25–26, 29
cultural resiliency model 26–27, 29

empirical evidence on race, culture and 29–31
structural destruction approach 27–28, 29
structural resiliency approach 28–29
white middle-class 7, 20, 28
see also education; poverty
Clawson, Dan 31, 46, 47
Clemetson, Lynette 19
Cohen, Patricia 26
Cohen, Philip 34
Collins, Patricia 8, 19, 27
communal societies 41, 43–44
Connidis, Ingrid A. 6
Cooney, Santana 20
Coser, Lewis and Rose 37, 38, 44
Crocker, Jill 31
cultural deficiency model 25–26, 29
cultural resiliency model 26–27, 29
Culture: Attitudes, values, norms, symbols, habits, and practices available to people
from the same society, institution, group, or organization which serve as a "tool
kit" (Swidler 2001) to interpret experiences and construct life strategies 8
empirical evidence on class, race and 29–31
and gender differences in carework 9–10
Latino/a 14–15, 20
marriage and 41–43
models to explain race differences in family experiences 24–27, 29
culture of poverty 14, 25, 26

D
Damaske, Sarah 19
Davies, Lorraine 6
"disorganization" argument 12–15, 18–19, 23, 25
divorce 30, 36, 43, 51
Dobson, James 2
Doing gender: "Activity of managing situated conduct in light of normative con-
ceptions of attitudes and activities appropriate for one's sex category" (West and
Zimmerman 1987: 127) 9–10
Duggan, Lisa 53
Durkheim, Émile 39

E
Edin, Kathryn 20, 24, 37, 49

education 30–31, 39, 49

Elving, Ronald 48

Epstein, Cynthia F. 7

Essentialism: A theory that attributes gender, racial/ethnic, or other social differences to biology, thus viewing these differences as deep and prevalent in all societies across time 7

Ettelbrick, Paula 53

Extended family: A residential or non-residential group of family members, related by blood, marriage or adoption, that includes relatives other than a mother, father, and minor children, such as adult children and their parents, siblings, grandparents and grandchildren, aunts, uncles, nieces and nephews, cousins, parents-in-law and siblings-in-law 1, 3–4

    gender differences in work to maintain 6

    marriage and ties to 37–38, 44–45

    men's involvement in 22, 23

    race and 21–23, 31

    social class and differences in experiences of 31–35

    "superorganization" of families of color 18–21, 25

    welfare reform working against 51

F

Familism: A set of beliefs that places high value on family and often places interests of the family ahead of those of an individual 14–15, 20, 25

Family and Medical Leave Act (FMLA) 1993 46–48

family, definitions of 2–3

family values 1–2

fathers 1, 19–20, 21

    welfare reform and biological 49–50

    work-life balance 5

Fictive kin: Individuals who are not related by blood, marriage, or legal adoption, but who nevertheless consider each other family members 2

Focus on the Family 2

Fowler, James 36

Frazier, E. Franklin 13

friends and neighbors 38–41

Furstenberg, Frank 49

G

Galinsky, Ellen 2

Gallagher, Sally 9, 10

gay and lesbian marriage 3, 45, 53

gender
    biases in discussions of work-life balance 5–6
    cultural views on 30
    differences in carework 6–10
    inequalities in welfare policies 49
    and FMLA 47
    norms in Latino/a society 14
Gerena, Mariana 22, 29
Gerson, Kathleen 11
Gerstel, Naomi 6, 9, 10, 22, 25, 29, 30, 31, 37, 38, 39, 46, 47
Goodwin, Jeff 44
Gornick, Janet 46
grandparents
    children living with 34
    providing care 6, 21, 29, 32
    social policies on 51–52
Greenstein, Theodore 10
Gubrium, Jaber 3
Gutman, Herbert 13

H
Hansen, Karen 34, 41
Hardesty, Monica 54
Harding, David 10
Haskins, Ron 14
Hays, Sharon 50
Heymann, Jody 6
Hochschild, Arlie 6, 10, 37
Holstein, James 3
honeymoons 41, 42
Huyser, Dana 31

I
immigrants 3–4, 27, 29
income, education and poverty rates by race 30–31
Institutionalization: The process of establishing a set of beliefs, values, practices, and social roles as a norm in a given social system (society as a whole or a specific organization), often accompanied by introduction of new laws or regulations and creation of formal mechanisms for implementation and enforcement of new rules 52

Intensive mothering: A term coined by Sharon Hays (1996) to refer to the contemporary dominant cultural ideology that dictates a child-centered, emotionally involving, and time-consuming approach to motherhood 7

J

Jackson, James 23
Jencks, Christopher 50
Journal of Marriage and Family 3

K

Kahn, Joan 9
Kaplan, Elaine 21
Kefalas, Maria 24, 37, 49
Kinkeeping: Activities that keep extended families together, such as providing care to relatives, organizing family gatherings, staying in touch, celebrating family events, mediating conflicts, and keeping others informed about family happenings 3, 6
Klempin, Serena 50

L

La Vida 14
Lamont, Michèle 10
Landry, Bart 19
Lareau, Annette 24
Latino/a families
    births to unmarried women 16, 18
    children living with a never married parent 16–17
    cultural deficiency model and 25
    cultural resiliency model and 26–27
    "disorganization" argument and 14–15
    familism in 14–15, 20, 25
    machismo and marianismo in 14, 19, 25
    marital status 15–16, 17–18
    structural destruction model and 27–28
    structural resiliency model and 29
    "superorganization" argument and 19
    and support for extended kin 22–23
Laub, John 44
Lempert, Lora B. 21
Letiecq, Bethany 52
Lewis, Oscar 14, 25

M

Macdonald, Cameron 51

machismo 14, 19, 25

marianismo 14, 25

marital status

    and involvement with neighbors and friends 38–39

    and involvement with parents and siblings 37–38

    by Latino/a subgroup 17–18

    by race and ethnicity 15–16

marriage xi, 36–45

    benefits of 36, 44

    championed by welfare policies 49–50

    and class differences 31

    communal societies and views on 41, 43–44

    contemporary expectations of 42

    costs of 37, 45

    cultural values and differing views on 30

    explanations for isolationist effects of 40–43

    and extended family ties 37–38, 44–45

    gay and lesbian 3, 45, 53

    as a "greedy institution" 37, 38

    and other social connections 38–40

    race and nuclear families 15–18

    self-selection processes in 36, 43

Matriarchal: Literally, the term means "the rule of mothers" and implies a society or a group (including familial group) where women, especially mothers, have power and authority and take on all the leadership roles; scholars disagree whether purely matriarchal societies ever existed 13, 14, 25

McAdam, Doug 44

McDonald, Katrina B. 21, 28

McGill, Brittany 9

McGonagle, Kate 47

McIntosh, Mary 37

Mead, Margaret 42

Medicaid 48–49

Mendez, Fernandez 26

Menjivar, Cecilia 27

Meyers, Marcia 46

Miller, Daniel 50

Mincy, Ronald 20, 24, 50

Mirandé, Alfredo 14, 19

Monroe, Pamela 50
Mothers
    Black 15–17, 18–19, 21
    and careers 5, 19
    Latino/a 14, 15–17, 18–19
    as "nurturer" 7–8
    teenage 21
    "welfare mothers" 50–51
    White 15–17, 42
    see also **Othermothers**; single mothers
Moynihan, Daniel Patrick 12–13, 14, 25
Musick, Marc 26
Mutchler, Jan 48

N
National Survey of Families and Households 29–30
The Negro Family 13
Nelson, Margaret 42
New York Times 5, 19, 26
New York Times Magazine 5
Newman, Katherine 20, 28–29
Nightingale, Demetra S. 50
Not-So-Nuclear Families 34, 41
Nuclear family: Family group consisting of a mother and a father who are married to each other and who co-reside with one another and their minor children; sometimes the term is applied to couples without children, single-parent families, or unmarried cohabiting couples with children 1, 42, 43
    black middle-class 19
    challenging norm of 18–19
    Latino/a 19
    race, marriage and 15–18
    social policy and 51, 54
    white middle-class 7, 20, 28
    widespread focus on 1–4, 46
nursing assistants 31, 32–33, 47

O
Obama, Barack 1, 48
Oliker, Stacey 51
Opting Out 5

Othermothers: Grandmothers, other female relatives, and non-relatives participating in a system of communal childrearing 20

P

parenting, class differences in 7–8
parents
    caring for elderly 30, 31, 37–38, 45, 48, 54
    of young children 41
Parker-Pope, Tara 5
Parsons, Talcott 3
Paschal, Angelia 20
Patriarchal: Literally, this term means "the rule of fathers" and refers to societies or groups (including families) where men as fathers are the primary authority figures who have power over women, children, and property; some use the term to refer to any form of male domination 14, 18
Patterson, Orlando 21, 25, 26
Pear, Robert 50
Perry-Jenkins, Maureen 34
Personal Responsibility and Work Opportunity Reconciliation Act (PRWORA) 1996 49
Pew Research Center 30, 31, 34, 51–52
physicians 31–32
Popenoe, David 3, 42
Porterfield, Fonda 52
poverty 27–28, 50–51
    culture of 14, 25, 26
    education and income rates by race 30–31
Powell, Brian 2
psychology 7–8, 40
Puerto Ricans 14, 18, 20
Putnam, Robert 44

R

race/ethinicity
    and cultural models to explain differences in family experiences 24–27, 29
    "disorganization" argument and families of color 12–15, 18–19, 23, 25
    education, income and poverty rates by 30–31
    empirical evidence on class, culture and 29–31
    and extended families 21–23, 31
    marriage and nuclear families 15–18

and structural models to explain differences in family experiences 24, 27–29

"superorganization" of families of color 18–21, 25

Raphael, Steven 50

Raspberry, William 12

Reciprocity: Norms and practices that involve getting something and providing something similar in return 20

"Reconsidering Culture and Poverty" 26

religion 39, 43–44

Riedmann, Agnes 6

Riley, Matilda 34

Rituals of Blood 21, 26

Rogler, Lloyd 20

Roschelle, Anne 21, 27

S

same-sex families 2–3, 9, 48

Sampson, Robert 44

Sarkisian, Natalia 9, 22, 25, 29, 30, 37, 38, 39

Schmidt, Heather 50

Self-selection effect: Difference between two (or more) groups that can be attributed to the ability of individuals to select themselves into one of these groups and makes it difficult to determine whether a certain process of interest created differences between groups, or whether these differences emerged because individuals were already different upon joining the group 36, 43

siblings 6, 33, 37–38, 43

single mothers

    among communities of color 14, 15, 19–20, 31

    nursing assistants and reliance on kin 33

    and support from biological fathers 50

    and "welfare policy" 36, 49–51

single people 38–39, 42, 44

Slater, Phillip 39

Small, Mario L. 10

Social capital: "The aggregate of the actual or potential resources which are linked to possession of a durable network of more or less institutionalized relationships of mutual acquaintance or recognition" (Bourdieu 1986: 248) 44

social policy and families 46–54

    Family and Medical Leave Act 46–48

    gay and lesbian marriage 53

    Medicaid 48–49

and policies on grandparents 51–52

"welfare" policies 49–51

Socialization: A set of "processes by which we learn and adapt to the ways of a given society or social group so as to adequately participate in it" (Handel, Cahill, and Elkin 2007) 8

Stacey, Judith 3, 48

Stack, Carol 20, 28, 34

Stoll, Michael 26

Stone, Pamela 5

structural destruction model 27–28, 29

structural resiliency model 28–29

Structure: Social arrangements that appear as material, objective, and external constraints and opportunities, frequently related to economic circumstances, which shape individuals' actions 8–9, 40–41

structural models to explain race differences in family experiences 24, 27–29

Sudarkasa, Niara 26, 27

"superorganization" argument 18–21, 25

Swidler, Ann 9

Swingle, Joseph 50

T

Tach, Laura 20, 24

Taylor, Robert 23

Temporary Assistance for Needy Families (TANF) 49, 50, 51

Tiller, Vicky 50

U

Underclass: This term, coined by anthropologist Oscar Lewis and developed (and contested) by many other scholars, typically refers to the most disenfranchised section of the population, persistently jobless or underemployed, with incomes below the poverty line 21, 28

The Unfinished Revolution 11

Universalism: Characteristic of a social policy that indicates that it benefits large sections of population and no one is excluded, which can be contrasted to "selective" policies that only benefit subgroups of the population based on their specific needs or other characteristics 47

U.S. Census Bureau 2, 17, 18, 30, 34

V

volunteering 39

20059438R00051

Made in the USA
Middletown, DE
14 May 2015